Head Figure Head:

The Search for the Hidden Life of Rick Perry

Glen Maxey

ISBN: 1468025988
ISBN-13: 978-1468025989

DEDICATION

To the courageous gay, lesbian, bisexual, transgendered and questioning
young people who will take up the cause and the fight
for full equality for our community.
Always remember what anthropologist Margaret Mead said:

Never doubt that a small group of thoughtful, committed citizens can
change the world; indeed, it's the only thing that ever has.

Go out and change the world.

ACKNOWLEDGMENTS

THANKS TO EVERYONE WHO ANSWERED THEIR EMAILS

CHEERS TO SPECTACULAR EDITORS

KUDOS TO THE LAWYERS

HAT TIP TO THE GRAPHICS GUY

A PLACE IN HEAVEN OR HELL (HIS CHOICE) TO MY PERSONAL LAWYER
WHO HELD MY HAND AND OTHER THINGS

A RELIEF FOR MY LEGION OF FRIENDS WHO NO LONGER
HAVE TO LISTEN TO ME TALK INCESSANTLY ABOUT THIS TOPIC

AND A VERY SPECIAL THANKS TO
"THE JOURNALIST"
WHO IS THE MOST PROFESSIONAL PERSON I'VE EVER WORKED WITH
AND IS ONE HECK OF AN INVESTIGATIVE REPORTER
(BUT MOST IMPORTANTLY HE BECAME MY FRIEND)

Glen Maxey

TABLE OF CONTENTS:

Introduction

One of the most discussed and dismissed rumors among Texas political types pertains to whether or not Rick Perry has had homosexual encounters. Most Capitol insiders heard the gossip about Geoff Connor and the rumored near-dissolution of Perry's marriage to Anita in 2003. Those of us who have been a part of Austin's GLBT community since the late 1980s have heard other men claim to have hooked up with the Governor. Newspapers and opposition researchers have tried to prove those connections for over a decade, but none of the supposed male partners or their confidantes wanted to go on the record about being fucked by Rick Perry—and inevitably face the scrutiny and public spotlight of a high-profile "outing."

Of course, millions of Texans are readily willing to admit they've been metaphorically fucked by Rick Perry. But few of them have stories that involve $200-an-hour hustlers.

When the rumors began recirculating in advance of Perry's presidential campaign announcement, journalists started poking into the old stories. Some reporters naturally called me, Glen Maxey, the first and only openly gay State Representative in Texas. I, in turn, activated my political and GLBT gossip circles and started compiling a list of two decades' worth of Rick's rumored tricks, and set out to find out the truth.

What began as idle curiosity on my part became an all-consuming investigation, fueled by Perry's growing hypocrisy on GLBT issues. For most of his career as a Legislator, Agriculture Commissioner, Lieutenant Governor and even Governor, Perry wasn't overtly anti-gay in his policies or rhetoric. He even signed a hate crimes act in Texas that had been killed in the Texas Senate at the request of the previous Governor, George W. Bush. Yet by 2005, Perry was using homophobia as a tool to pander to the religious right, staging an elaborate signing ceremony for Texas' ban on same-sex marriage. The hypocrisy of Perry's blatant efforts to use the lives of GLBT Texans as a political wedge issue while he himself was rumored to be engaging in clandestine homosexual encounters provided ample motivation for me to keep digging and pushing until these stories come to light.

Through my initial investigation, Perry's campaign ramped up and he surged to the lead in the national polls. That further complicated matters: suddenly potential sources thought they had a story to sell. Why should they tell me when some tabloid might pay a higher price? Before I could get my best source, his lawyers, and a publisher to come to terms, Perry plummeted in the polls. By the time he couldn't remember the third federal agency he'd eliminate, my story seemed dead in the water. Rick Perry managed to singlehandedly strangle his own campaign, and in the process he more or less smothered my potential tell-all about his homosexual proclivities.

What follows is the story of my failed efforts to expose Rick Perry's homosexual encounters in the national press. It's the tale of simple curiosity aroused by a reporter's questions about a past alleged sexual scandal and of how complicated it is to find the answers to those questions. Over the course of my efforts to discover Rick Perry's secret homosexual past, I learned a lot about not only many of his alleged former partners, but also the difficulty in exposing them to the wider public, particularly in a state where so many individuals' jobs and livelihoods depend on not incurring the wrath of Texas' longest-serving governor and his massive network of cronies, appointees, and henchmen.

It's also the tale of the growing visibility of the GLBT movement in Texas, and the tension between the right to privacy of public figures and the potential forfeiture of privacy when hypocrisy about sexuality is used as a political tool.

When I started my investigation, the first question I asked myself was, "Can I prove that Rick Perry has had sex with men?" The second question I asked was, "Will I ever be able to share this research widely enough to affect the candidacy of a hypocritical candidate?"

Because you are reading this, you just became at least a part of the answer to the latter question.

Part I: The Approach.

Late in the spring of 2011, an editor at National News Outlet read an article on Politico.com that mentioned the old rumors about Rick Perry's sexuality and how those stories would resurface if he ran for President. The editor had been told about these rumors a political conference, so when he read that Perry's team was "more than prepared for a re-airing of unsubstantiated rumors," that was like waving a red flag in front of an angry bull.

<u>My Coming Out Story</u>

But before we delve into stories about Perry's homosexual encounters, first let me provide some background on my own place in Texas GLBT history. In 2003 I retired after six terms as the first (and still only) openly gay State Representative in Texas. Before holding office, back in the mid 1980s I was a closeted legislative aide for a Texas State Senator, Oscar H. Mauzy. At the time HIV and AIDS had exploded on the scene, roiling up considerable political turmoil in conservative Texas. From my closet, I had stepped out slightly to become an activist, but initially only to help the first men in Austin who were identified as infected. In late 1985 the Commissioner of the Texas Department of Health called for a new rule allowing for the permanent quarantine of Texans "suspected of being infected" with this new gay related immune deficiency, later to become known as HIV and AIDS.

My boss represented Oak Lawn, the Dallas gay ghetto. When gay leaders in Dallas called Senator Mauzy for help blocking this rule, I handled their calls. When I told Mauzy that someone needed to organize the opposition to the TDH rule proposal, the Senator replied dryly, "That someone is you."

I organized the hearing before the Texas Department of Health, and we won the issue. The proposal was withdrawn. That result garnered lots of press, and I stepped in front of a bank of national network television cameras to talk about the victory. Later that night, while watching the news, I was shocked to see "Glen Maxey, Gay Activist" in yellow letters superimposed over my chest. I had, in a flash, been outed to the nation, to the Senator, to my own mother, and everyone I knew. Sen. Mauzy was running for the Texas Supreme Court in 1986, and at the end of the year I would be out of a job when his Senate term ended. In the ensuing weeks, every job offer I had from other State Senators evaporated. In Texas in 1986, "gay activist" was not a prime job qualification.

When you are given lemons, you make lemonade. Seemingly overnight I went from being a closeted staffer to being the leading openly gay GLBT activist in Texas. Within a year, local gay and lesbian leaders from across Texas formed an advocacy group. When our organization needed a staffer, I stepped forward and was hired as the first full-time lobbyist and Executive Director of the Lesbian/Gay Rights Lobby of Texas—now Equality Texas.

Around the same time our GLBT political movement started in Texas, Rick Perry was elected to the Legislature and came to Austin in 1985 as a new Democratic State Representative from a rural west Texas district centered around Haskell County, Texas. I noticed him, but not because of his politics or stature. For the most part, Perry was a small-town cotton farmer and legislative back-bencher. What I do remember distinctly is that I thought he was the hottest, tightest-Wrangler-wearing cowboy legislator that a closeted gay guy would want to have around as eye candy. In fact, in 1989 I participated in a straw poll with the female lobbyists (being, naturally, the only openly gay male lobbyist at the time) to pick the legislator with the best buns. I nominated Perry, and he won unanimously.

But back to the story at hand.

First Contact

The editor at National News Outlet assigned a reporter, hereafter "The Journalist," to check out the rumors and stories about Perry's sexual dalliances. Having already built a solid reputation as a determined investigative reporter, The Journalist was just the person to doggedly chase down decades-old rumors about the potential GOP candidate's past. He started with an old blog post on *Burnt Orange Report*, a website started by University of Texas students. In 2004 *BOR* detailed rumors surrounding Perry's homosexual encounters. (The post has since been deleted.) The Journalist contacted *BOR*'s current publisher, Karl-Thomas Musselman, who referred him to me.

When my phone rang, I was relaxing in my small apartment in Central Austin. It was The Journalist, who was calling to ask what I knew about Perry's sexual past. I offered to tell him what little I knew, adding that the stories had already been told to dozens of reporters since the 2004 *BOR* post and to various opposition researchers, most recently during the 2010 gubernatorial campaign, when Bill White ran a tough campaign against Perry but still came up short.

My answer to The Journalist was, "I know two things. I know the same things that everyone else has heard about Rick Perry, Geoff Connor, and Anita Perry's divorce attorney. And I know what random gay men told me in late 1989 and 1990."

Ancient Gay History

By 1990, I was the most prominent and visible GLBT activist in Texas. I was on television almost weekly addressing GLBT issues and engaging in huge debates on HIV/AIDS legislation at the Capitol. About this time, I was also volunteering for the efforts in Travis County (which includes Austin) to support Ann Richards's gubernatorial campaign.

As I told The Journalist, during those early years of public GLBT advocacy, on multiple occasions gay men asked me about Rick Perry while I was out socializing and networking in local gay bars. They would always start with something like: "Hey, aren't you Glen Maxey, the guy who works at the Capitol?" After I confirmed my identity, they followed with an oft-repeated inquiry: "Do you know a representative named Rick Perry?" I'd reply that I did, often with a comment about his bubble butt or some other gay-oriented remark. They responded in several ways. "Well, I'm messing around with him." Or, "My friend is hooking up with him." This happened at least four times in Austin's newly opened gay bar, Oil Can Harry's, and I distinctly remember the men calling Rick Perry by name.

Because my policy was (and still is) not to "out" people, and Rick Perry was at the time a harmless legislator as far as the gay Lobby was concerned, I would always reply "lucky you" or some other dish remark. It never occurred to me to note the guys' names and I don't remember any of them being men known to me before the conversations.

I told The Journalist these stories and said I would give him a call if anything else came to mind. But his inquiry planted a seed. I thought about Perry's decidedly right-wing detour since his first term as Governor, his growing anti-GLBT agenda and willingness to use the community as a wedge political issue, and his willingness to associate himself with people and organizations that have a history of inflaming bigotry against GLBT individuals. I started to wonder what I could do to find the evidence supporting the truth of the two stories. If anyone had the Rolodex and gay gossip network to prove these rumors, it was me. I have been around Texas politics for over forty years. I had worked on over a hundred campaigns, from precinct chair to President, worked as an aide to two Texas Senators, as a gay-rights lobbyist, and served six terms in the Legislature. (I had even been elected as the last Travis County Inspector of Hides and Animals in 1986. I ran as a lark, succeeding the previous inspector, who had been elected 90 years earlier in 1896—then I helped abolish the office.)

To put it mildly, I know a lot of GLBT people, political activists, and Texas Capitol denizens. So that afternoon, after the Journalist's call, I began making a list of people to ask about Rick Perry rumors. At the top of the list were people I knew at the Capitol from 1985 to the present who were closeted back then, just as I was. The list included reporters, legislators, staffers, lobbyists, and more. Political gossip is the currency of a legislative body. After decades had passed and people had moved on or retired, I figured they would be willing to talk or share what they knew.

That same day, June 23, 2011, I sent the first of my series of investigative emails through Facebook:

> What do you know about Perry's homosexual dalliances?
>
> I'm working with a journalist on as story about all of Rick Perry's gay rumors (and there many). I'm throwing a wide net, asking folks around in the 80's and 90's period, if they remember any stories that were even just told in passing.

The narrative that follows from here is what spooled out of almost 3000 ensuing emails and text messages I exchanged over the next five months, with everyone from lawmakers to hustlers to lawyers to lobbyists (of course sometimes it's hard to distinguish between the groups).

I tell the story from this point in first person. I will use the original emails and texts as much as possible to track the steps in my investigation. To honor the common request not to unduly expose innocent bystanders in this story, I use some pseudonyms and made-up nicknames in place of real names, such as "Legislative Insider" or "James the Jogger." All pseudonyms are introduced in quotation marks. Where I replaced names in the original source emails and texts, I have used brackets.

I've omitted many of the thousands of email exchanges, some of which were uninteresting dead ends and others of which might needlessly injure someone's reputation or "out" people who don't want to be outed or involved in reports concerning the sexual activities of a presidential candidate. I've left the texts and emails in uncorrected and unedited form, save for minor typographical corrections.

The story generally flows chronologically to describe the process by which I sought to investigate Perry's homosexual proclivities and the results of my search. The effort included hundreds of telephone exchanges, interviews, storytellings, and lots of laughter, frustration, and angst. Many leads went nowhere. Several leads presented the most improbable of coincidences. And after all of the research is said and done, after weeks of contacts, hundreds of hours of interviews, and thousands of exchanges, I suppose I'm either a great amateur investigative reporter or simply a persevering gay gossip queen. You decide which.

Part II: Casual Encounters

My early emails resulted in responses that included a surprisingly large volume and variety of Perry innuendo. Some stories I heard repeatedly from multiple sources. Other rumors set off on winding investigative trails as I tracked down a friend-of-a-friend who'd heard a story at a party…. Along the way, as word of my inquiries spread, friends and colleagues reached out with stories and long-forgotten gossip that provided a seemingly endless series of leads. Not all of those leads panned out, but some turned into major sources.

I'll start with the most commonly told story, and the one that almost exposed Perry in the first place.

Geoff Connor

Without fail, when I asked most people if they knew anything about Rick Perry's rumored same-sex encounters, the most common response I got was about the Geoff Connor story. Connor was the former Secretary of State, with whom Perry was rumored to have had a long-ranging affair. Connor had worked as an attorney in the Agricultural Department when Perry was Ag Commissioner. When Perry took over as Governor in January of 2001, Connor was appointed Assistant Secretary of State (SOS). Perry then appointed Connor as Secretary of State in September 2003.

Here's a typical version I heard of the Connor-Perry rumors as told and retold and spun by many sources:

In late 2003, Perry's wife Anita walked in on her husband with Connor in the Governor's mansion. Anita left the mansion and went directly to the opulent Driskill Hotel, built by Texas cattle baron Col. Jesse Driskill in 1886.

The next day, Anita's coworkers at the Texas Association Against Sexual Assault heard her talking loudly on the phone. The paraphrased conversation was that she had made comments like: "You promised it wouldn't happen again." "You said you wouldn't see Geoff again." "I can't live this way." She said she was hiring a high profile divorce attorney. Somehow a pre-divorce-suit financial settlement and reconciliation were achieved.

In political Austin, gossip is gold. Trading intel on the Connor story became a popular pastime in the Capitol and surrounding bars. Media outlets used the rumors as a heuristic to launch their own speculation. But none were able to provide sufficient proof of Perry's encounter—with Connor or otherwise—to justify a genuine expose.

The story became so widespread that Perry's handlers finally invited Ken Herman of the *Austin American-Statesman* to do a one-on-one interview with the Governor. In the resulting article, Herman recounted Perry's discussion with him concerning his marriage and his relationship with Anita. Perry denied that the marriage had any problems. In his report of the interview, Herman did not mention Connor, or that the rumors focused on a homosexual encounter. Perry used the interview as an opportunity to deny the story fully. Moreover, Perry put the blame on Democrats and sleaze politics. Unfortunately, no one in the fourth estate pursued the rumors much after that. Herman helped Perry put the Connor story to bed, at least in the sense that no one was going to print anything further, now that the Governor had publicly denied it.

On the other hand, to be fair, neither Herman nor the straight Texas press had a fraction of my contacts among Texas gay politicos who would be willing to talk to them. So it was not an easy story for them to investigate. It was not easy for me either. This is still Texas, after all—and even Austin ain't quite San Francisco. The Republican and lobby-controlled state government and courts in Texas can still make this an unfriendly and sometimes dangerous place for gays. Outing a powerful homosexual Texas Republican officeholder who doesn't want to be outed is, as they say in East Texas, "harder than eatin' red beans with a pitchfork."

The Connor story, and Connor, mostly dropped from public view. In December 2004, Connor resigned as Secretary of State to pursue private sector activities. His resignation came just before the beginning of the 2005 Texas Legislative session. The Texas Legislature meets for 140 days in odd-numbered years. The office of the Secretary of State requires confirmation by the Texas Senate. Because the Senate had not been in session since Connor's appointment, that confirmation would have come up during the 2005 session. Any Senator could have grilled Connor under oath.

Anita never filed for divorce.

In 2008, the Governor's mansion burned almost to the ground in an arson. Since then, Rick and Anita have been living in a rental mansion (costing taxpayers $10,000 a month) in a cushy neighborhood in a gated community. And it has not escaped the notice of Austin's ladies who lunch that while she publicly stood by her man in the following eight years, she rarely smiled in campaign photo-ops. (That would strangely shift when Perry entered the Presidential primary.)

As I started digging, I heard versions of the above story time and again. But I also heard some new information.

Some of my friends and acquaintances reached out to their own networks, fueling the gay community speculation with the growing sense that Perry would run for President and that these rumors would resurface. One friend emailed me about a man she met at a conference. He was from the same small hometown as Anita Perry and told my friend that some folks back home believed that Perry was indeed a homosexual, and that rumors of Anita's hiring the high profile divorce attorney had spread back home.

My early rumor-sleuthing with politicos was easily lubricated by regular late-night alcohol-fueled gatherings that drew old timers and young folks alike. One such gathering was on the final Friday of each month. For years, that gathering was hosted by the late Molly Ivins at her home. It continues to this day in the homes of various liberals around Austin. Many of the regular attendees date back to the Ann Richards era, if not decades before. Now that Perry's presidential campaign was on the rise, they were more than happy to share old rumors.

A family lawyer friend of mine knew an employee in the high profile divorce attorney's office at the time of the supposed split and negotiations. The friend asked the lawyer's employee and was told "I cannot comment." The family lawyer said her friend's tone suggested the response was not exactly a denial. If there were no truth to the widespread rumor, why wouldn't the lawyer's employee have said that? I understand that lawyer-client communications are confidential and privileged. But non-communications by non-existent non-clients aren't. Again and again in my investigation and inquiries, I encountered stories of odd non-denials. Those repeated non-denials were part of the challenge of delving into Perry's secret life. People who didn't answer "yes" to questions had ways to imply with tone of voice or a head nod that the answer was hardly "no." But that's challenging to document.

Much of the Connor material I encountered was not new—it was just repetition of what I and many others had heard before: many stories, many "friend of a friend" instances of retellings of the alleged Connor incidents.

Joey the Hustler

What immediately pulled me into the investigation more deeply and strongly than anything else was the story of "Joey," a hustler who had told his friends a story about hooking up with Perry on multiple occasions.. Joey became a central focus of my obsessive inquiry, as his story became the holy grail in my search for the truth about Perry's alleged homosexual relationships.

I first heard about Joey on June 23th, shortly after I received the first phone call from The Journalist. His questions about Perry inspired me to start digging around Facebook. I immediately got two independent responses, one from "Capitol Reporter," who was widely respected, and another from "Capitol Insider," who had intimate knowledge of the goings-on in state government, and put me in touch with his contact, "Gay Businessman."

Facebook Chat 6/23/2011 2:00 PM To Capitol Reporter

Glen: A reporter just called me about Rick Perry's hookups. Being around the Capitol through his time there, do you know anything about Perry?

Capitol Reporter: If I knew anything other than Geoff Connor I'd have written a column for the Huffington Post!

Glen: LOL. So you don't know anything?

Capitol Reporter: Funny you ask. A mutual friend of ours, [Gay Businessman], told me a wild story of a hustler named [Joey] he met who talked about hooking up wth Perry.

Glen: Wow. I'll give him a call right now. You have his number?

Capitol Reporter: Sure.

Just a few hours later, I hit gold again:

Facebook Chat from Capitol Insider

Capitol Insider: It's really funny that you've asked. I was at a dinner party about six months ago where I met a guy who told me an outrageous story about knowing a hustler who had hooked up with Perry on multiple occasions.

Glen: Wow. Think he'd talk to a reporter? Can you call him? At least see if he knows the hustler's name? See if it's [Joey]. I wonder if this is the same guy? What's the chances that the first two people I've asked both know somebody who knows a gay hustler. Amazing.

Capitol Insider: Let me call him. Not promising anything, but it won't hurt to try.

In short, two of the first people I reached out on the very first day came back with independent stories about Perry and a gay hustler. What were the odds? This is what really hooked me into the story.

I then contacted Gay Businessman, the friend of Capitol Insider, to see what he remembered. Here's his response:

EMAIL 6/23/2011 11:52 PM From Gay Businessman

The whole story is that i have a ex friend who hired this kid years ago for sex and they became friends. I was out at Rain [a gay club in Austin] with my friend and we ran into this hustler kid. He very matter of factly stated that he had just been hired to spend the weekend at the Driskill with Perry and an assistant of Perrys. He was non chalant about it and said that it happened 3 or 4x a year and he gave some sexual details about Perry and the other guy. This was in the early 2000s like maybe 03. This guy who said all this is still on [a popular website] promoting his "services." He is late 20s by now or maybe even 30. I know his real first name but would have to do a little digging to find his screen name

Gay Businessman did some Internet searching and quickly came up with Joey's screen name used on the hustler websites. I asked a young computer wiz friend of mine to search the internet for Joey. Ten minutes later, he had located multiple listings for Joey, who apparently traveled around to various Texas cities throughout the year plying his trade.

With very little effort, we found photos of Joey, a phone number, and several email addresses. I was amazed. This was my email message to The Journalist—just two days after he first contacted me:

EMAIL 6/24/2011 1:12 AM To The Journalist from Glen

Subject: Summation before I sleep.

So we have [Gay Businessman] ready to talk to you about his conversation with a hustler named [Joey.] We have numerous sites with the hustler's name and phone and more explicit stuff.

[Capitol Insider] is going to try to track down his source for his recent rumor re: a hustler, who ironically was also named [Joey.]

Pretty good detective work for someone whose memory sucks.

The Journalist called these sources the very next day, trying to pin down whether both Joeys were the same hustler.

Dead-End Leads

Not all of my leads panned out.

A friend at a party told me that former Texas Democratic Party Chair Charles Soechting might have some information. Soechting's name had appeared in news articles about the Perry rumors after he publicly referred to the rumors at a political rally in 2004. With the story gaining new life because of Perry's reported presidential ambitions, Soechting was apparently retelling old tales again. He also told about people he knew who supposedly saw Perry going in and out of a young man's apartment late at night. Soechting was a former Department of Public Safety (DPS) officer, so I speculated that he might have known the DPS officers assigned to guard Perry, but Soechting never confirmed this.

I spoke to Soechting. He knew of a Hispanic man named "Tommy" who supposedly attended parties with Perry. But Soechting couldn't remember Tommy's last name. Soechting reviewed some old opposition research in his files, but that turned up nothing.

But talking with Soechting, I wondered if his DPS connection was the source of the rumors. If Perry had had late night encounters, almost certainly he would have taken his guard detail with him. DPS officers are never to leave the Governor alone. It's nearly impossible to slip away from them. (Former aides to Ann Richards told me a story about the time she once tried—and failed.)

Another friend, "Bill," told me that he had a lady friend who'd gossiped about a male friend of hers supposedly hooking up with Perry. Bill reached out to his contact and tried just to get the name of her friend. She said the man's name was "Joseph"—and she said that he was a professional. I wondered if we'd hit on yet another connection to Joey the Hustler. But it turned out her friend was a professional of the white-collar kind, and she wasn't going to pursue our inquiry. The Journalist and I harangued Bill for weeks to get her to talk. Bill pressed her, but it became increasingly clear she wanted to be left alone. We dropped that lead. It's hard to blame a friend for wanting to protect her source from the harsh light of outing a Governor.

I also reached out to a friend, "AIDS Educator," who works at an AIDS awareness group. He soon emailed me back with a story about a man named "Calvin", who worked at "Large Tech Firm," a prominent software company in Austin.

EMAIL 7/14/2011 10:01 PM From "AIDS Educator"

Got some more info on [Calvin]. I had the story a little bit wrong. Here's the corrected info and some new as well. He did work at [Large Tech Firm] in the late 1990s, and 1997 is probably the year that he left. After he or his partner allegedly had sex with Perry, his partner, who worked for the government (not sure which level of government or anything) was forced to resign, and it was at that time that [Calvin] left Austin and they moved to Oklahoma or Kansas.

I searched Facebook, Google, and LinkedIn and I found two potential Calvins. Both had what I thought to be the correct last name. The most promising was a now an Austin massage therapist who had a review on his website mentioning how much folks at Large Tech Firm looked forwarded to the days he would do chair massages at their site. The Journalist followed these trails but neither panned out. Eventually I dropped that lead as well.

Bob's Friend

Working my network, I got in touch with the partner of a deceased GLBT leader who had worked in the same building where the Department of Agriculture was located at the time when Perry was Ag Commissioner. While the partner never knew anything firsthand, he connected me to a former county employee, "Bob." Bob said a friend of his had claimed back in 1998 that he was hooking up with Rick Perry on the side.

Bob said that he had hung out with the friend for a while but the relationship hadn't developed as he had hoped. During that time, Bob noticed that the guy often had new clothes and jewelry. Because the guy worked at the mall in a low paying job, Bob was curious how he was affording it.

"My sugar daddy is buying it for me," Bob remembered him saying.

"Who's your sugar daddy?" Bob asked.

The guy demurred. Bob pressed him. "You won't know him," the guy said. "He's a state bureaucrat." Asked again, he replied, "He's the Agriculture Commissioner, Rick Perry."

Bob said, "Of course I know who he is, he's running for Lieutenant Governor!"

Bob had lost touch with the friend, but within a few minutes of searching on Facebook, we found him. As usual in these searches, we had dozens of mutual Facebook friends. We reached out, and he denied the entire story.

Underwear, Shorts, and Jogging

I heard stories about Perry prancing around in his "most inappropriate" underwear in his apartment shared with other legislators during a special legislative session, a story about Perry in a hot tub with young male Capitol tour guides, and an anecdote about Perry at the UT pool in a speedo.

But more than anything, on the fashion front, I kept hearing stories about his running shorts. One former elected official used to take his son to the same barbershop as Perry would take his son in West Austin. The former elected official would laugh at the Governor's predilection for sporting short jogging shorts, as well as shaved arms *and* legs.

Another gay friend said Perry would "cruise" him and his partner at the Blockbuster by the UT campus, again in his short shorts.

I heard other stories from men who jogged on the trail around Lady Bird Lake in central Austin, the most popular trail in town. Perry would chat up men on the trail about their MP3 players or some such. Many friends seemed to have a story about another friend who saw Perry at the water station by Austin High School, where he apparently would hitch his leg up to "stretch" at such an angle that his short shorts left nothing to the imagination. A campaign staffer told me a story about a running buddy who was talking about a pulled groin muscle at the water station in front of Perry. Perry allegedly pulled up his shorts, exposing his junk as if on purpose, and said "I pulled one way up here."

Coyote Legend

Perry's coyote-shooting story—a tale he told on the 2010 campaign trail, that he killed a coyote while jogging, with a gun stowed in his short shorts—struck me as funny by comparison. He was jogging with a laser sighted .380 Ruger pistol? A metrosexual handgun, by Texas standards. He carried a gun because he was afraid of snakes? In February? When snakes are hibernating or moving slowly? He must really, really be afraid of snakes. Of course, they're so long and sinuous! He's lucky no one pulled one out at a presidential debate. And then he shot a little coyote ("song dog," as our Native Americans call them) because he was afraid it would attack him or his dog? And no evidence, no photos, no police report back up his story? And where were the DPS detail? Wouldn't they have made some report since shooting a gun in the city is illegal? Did he have a concealed weapon permit? And where did he conceal it? I learned that wide-ranging open records requests had been submitted to state and local agencies asking for documentation of the alleged shooting—and the agencies produced nothing.

That sounds a lot harder to prove than the many stories of his alleged homosexual encounters.

Straight Reporters Investigating Gays

I'd relate these stories back to The Journalist, who at times didn't understand the lingo.

EMAIL 6/27/2011 3:25 PM To The Journalist

another capitol friend would only confirm that Perry would always cruise him and his partner when shopping in his jogging shorts in the neighborhood. Don't think that gets us there. LOL

EMAIL 6/27/2011 3:25 PM From The Journalist

Cruise? Like hit on?

EMAIL 6/27/2011 3:26 PM To The Journalist

I think that would only be the "unspoken stares at the crotch" kinda cruise.

Are you gay? Maybe my weak gay humor jokes aren't making sense if you're not.

EMAIL 6/27/2011 3:32 PM From The Journalist

Not gay. But thought there might be more to the cruise than that. If it helps, I did LOL. Jogging shorts are always funny.

As I mentioned above, the Journalist's position outside of the gay subculture was important for another reason.

Reporter after reporter had tried to source the rumors that Perry engaged in homosexual encounters. They all failed, because none of them had the trust of the GLBT community. Even most other politicos lacked access to the network of open and closeted Capitol staffers and officials that I regularly traded information with, let alone the wider network of gay Austin. Back in my days as a legislator, a female colleague used to question how I'd always know the scheming at work behind a bill. I'd say, "You can't talk in front of a waiter or male hair dresser in this town without it getting back to me."

Many people seemed to tell me everything they knew, because they could trust me to keep their names out of the final news story. I'd tell them to expect a call from The Journalist and that it was OK to repeat the stories to him if he said he would protect their identities. But when I would confer with The Journalist later about what the sources said, I realized that people would water down what they told National News Outlet, unsure if it was really off the record or not. That didn't surprise me too much—for most of us, talking to a friend is different than talking to a journalist.

As our investigation continued and our working relationship deepened, The Journalist would often express frustration about the difficulty of getting these men to tell their stories or go on the record. After I had sent him the following message, he'd often ask if I'd follow up his calls where he'd hit a brick wall and give them my "Rosa Parks story."

EMAIL 7/21/2011 5:24 PM To The Journalist

Great work.

I feel for [James]. It's takes guts to come out as a gay person, still in these days. Not so much to friends, but to deal with your parents, grandparents, relatives, etc. To be put in the national spotlight for a casual homo sex act takes a lot of balls.

Some how you've gotta give him a feeling that the pain / shame of this is an act of courage that will help improve the GLBT community in the long run. It will help block someone with an evil agenda for us in the community. It will embarrass the antigay religious bigots who have aligned themselves with Perry. It sends a message to lots of others about using the GLBT community as a political wedge issue and a scapegoat in their campaigns.

While he doesn't realize it, it could be the most important thing a person could do for the GLBT community at this point in history.

Every time I've had to step up as a gay person and do something like this I just remember what the famed anthropologist Margaret Meade said:

"A small group of thoughtful people could change the world. Indeed, it's the only thing that ever has."

He needs to know that most every hero and heroine did his/her thing that changed the world as an INDIVDUAL action.

Rosa Parks wasn't at a tea party with a bunch of friends. She was sitting there all alone.

Former Legislator

The Journalist and I were still working to get people to go on the record about what they knew about Perry's same-sex encounters. Short on sources with firsthand knowledge, we were collecting mostly stories from friends and colleagues of the people who claimed they *had* slept with him. It wasn't perfect, but at some point when a significant portion of an individual's social network goes on the record with a major publication to state that their friend professed to have fucked the Governor, well... where there's that much smoke, there's likely some secret sexual fire. Such was the case of "Former Legislator," whose friends were very willing to repeat his tales.

EMAIL 6.27.11 8:24 PM Email from retired graphics guy

> I always heard that [Former Legislator] had admitted that he and Perry and [Another Legislator] were all getting it on, and I thought I heard that there was something in print about it, but I've never seen it.

Former Legislator had been outed in criminal court proceedings. He'd been indicted in the late 1980s of misappropriating funds from a trade organization and giving the funds to his gay lover, "Arthur." During the trial, the judge sent the jury out of the room to discuss whether or not it was admissible to disclose the relationship between Former Legislator and Arthur. To this day, GLBT status is not protected in Texas—one can be fired for admitting to being gay. In the 1980s most Texas gays were understandably very reluctant to put this information in depositions, affidavits, or other legal documents.

At the time of Former Legislator's trial, in Texas it was still illegal to engage in homosexual acts. Admitting to a physical relationship was legally prejudicial. Instead, during the trial while the jury was out of the room, the judge instructed that the alleged homosexual relationship between Former Legislator and Arthur could be referred to only as a "romantic" relationship. Former Legislator later appealed his conviction, in part, on the grounds that even the reference to a "romantic" relationship between him and his alleged male romantic interest unfairly prejudiced the jury against the Legislator defendant.

In any case, I knew Former Legislator was living in San Antonio. I had seen him in years past with a man I presumed to be his lover at GLBT events and political fundraisers, so I worked my San Antonio network to see what I could turn up. My first call was to a well-known member of the GLBT community, "San Antonio Gay Activist." He told me he heard the story about the Former Legislator and Perry in the late 1990s from another gay leader. San Antonio Gay Activist mentioned two other friends of the Former Legislator, both now living outside of San Antonio. I worked my networks to find contact information for them. I found a few people on Facebook with the same name, and started reaching out to see if they were friends of Former Legislator.

EMAIL 7/11/2011 7:13 PM To The Journalist

Subject: Former Legislator

I found one gay in Fort Lauderdale on Facebook... Hopefully, he'll respond soon if i have the right guy. he's the guy [San Antonio Gay Activist] said told him that [Former Legislator] had told him that he'd had affair with Rick.

EMAIL 7/11/2011 6:56 PM To San Antonio Gay Activist

Subject: Perry and his gay side

I'm working with a national news outlet on a story about all Perry's gay stuff. We have lots of leads but just trying to get some bullets. It's pretty clear that Perry and [Former Legislator] had an affair back in the 80's.

We can't run with it unless [Former Legislator] at least denies it. He won't answer the phone.
A source says he told [name redacted] in Florida about the hookup.

Do you or anyone you know have any good phone number for [name redacted] in Florida? or where in Florida he moved?

Thanks for anything you can do to help us tie up this one.

My friend in San Antonio confirmed that I had the right Facebook profile, and it turned out I had a Facebook friend in common with Former Legislator's friend in Florida. What are the odds? This way I was able to reach two close friends of Former Legislator.

EMAIL 7/12/2011 10:45 AM From The Journalist

Subject: hey

I talked to [Former Legislator]'s friend in Florida. He went on the record and said that [Former Legislator] never told him directly that he hooked up with perry but [Former Legislator] implied that he knew that Perry was gay.

I was able to speak personally with one of Former Legislator's friends, who had moved elsewhere in the state. He told me that Former Legislator had told him the story of his first encounter with Perry in great detail: it had been at a legislative conference somewhere in the northwest (perhaps Seattle, he didn't remember exactly). The two had been drinking and stumbled back to Former Legislator's room. The key point in the story for me was when it was recounted that Former Legislator said Perry was nonchalant when leaving the next morning. "It was clear that this wasn't Rick's first rodeo," the friend recalled Former Legislator as saying.

EMAIL 7/12/2011 2:04 PM To San Antonio Gay Activist

[Former Legislator's friend] confirmed that [Former Legislator] told him directly that he'd had sex with Perry.

[Name Redacted] in Florida confirmed that [Former Legislator] didn't tell him he had sex with Rick, but told him [Former Legislator] knew for sure that Rick was gay

Since we still don't have a confirmation nor denial from [Former Legislator,] the next best thing is to get some additional folks that he told.

Any ideas of guys who were/are friends of his? or just guys on the cocktail, social circuit that he socialized with?

Thanks.

Now we seemed to have another solid story for The Journalist's article. I looked up Former Legislator on Facebook to find more leads.

EMAIL 7/12/2011 8:48 PM To Journalist

it's pretty weird that he only has a dozen friends or so.

And even weirder, one of my former organizers on the Howard Dean campaign, [Mark], shows up on there. I sent an email to [Mark] asking if he had a cell phone number for [Former Legislator]. Just seeing what he says.

Pretty sure that that boy is straight. But maybe not. Not that I'm assigning anything to the fact that [Mark] and [Former Legislator] would be Facebook friends. LOL

EMAIL 7/12/2011 9:06 PM From The Journalist

I couldn't find [Former Legislator] on facebook. Not that my fingers are broken.... I just don't think he uses Facebook. He's got no activity on it. And 12 friends. it's pretty hard to be on facebook with so little friends.

I chatted through Facebook with Mark, who told stories of attending "gay parties" with Former Legislator, and being wined and dined by him. Mark told me, "I never knew who his partner(s) were. He seemed like he was in the closet, although he was always introducing me to other gay men and inviting me to parties where I was the only one who wasn't gay. He never mentioned [that he was gay specifically] but doesn't put much effort into hiding it."

My young friend Mark had one other helpful tip – "He likes to drink and talk. Maybe a daytime call from a reporter isn't the best way to get it out of him." Maybe all I needed to do was just send a cute young guy with a bottle of whiskey over to Former Legislator's house and chat him up.

In his interviews with Texas politicos, The Journalist was told multiple times about legal filings that would mention Perry and The Former Legislator. Parallel to my gossip sleuthing, I tried to track down court filings pertaining to the Former Legislator's divorce and criminal case, and other potential legal documents. I'd heard that the Legislator's wife told about the affair in their divorce pleadings, and that there was evidence of purloined funds used for travel with and gifts to Perry in the criminal court proceedings.

I started with a search for the Former Legislator's divorce, which in Texas would be granted by the county in which they filed for it. I searched where they lived; I searched Travis County; I searched major urban areas—nothing. I even searched the Bureau of Vital Statistics, but was unable to prove they were divorced, let alone find the filing.

I turned my attention to the criminal case, which was filed right here in Austin. Those public records were easy enough to locate. The Journalist offered to provide funds for document reproduction. After much trouble and frustration, not to mention confronting seven gigantic boxes of unorganized legal papers, this route was determined to be a bust.

Because I could never find a divorce filing, I opined to The Journalist that I was willing to bet they never even got a divorce.

The Journalist interviewed Former Legislator on several occasions by phone. Former Legislator denied the affair outright to him. During one of the final interviews, The Journalist acted on my suggestion and asked him "Where did you file your divorce?" His reply, "We aren't divorced."

So much for that. I knew that technically, my failure to find the filings did not mean they had not filed for divorce or had not separated or had not consulted divorce lawyers. But I never found evidence of a divorce.

Two Guys in a Field of Bluebonnets

Bluebonnets are the state flower in Texas. In the Spring, they blanket the roadsides in Central Texas, and young families stop their cars and carefully position toddlers in the pools of blue for gorgeous photos destined for the family album. Nothing is cuter or prettier.

And nothing, absolutely guaran-damn-teed nothing, is more homosexual in Texas than two buffed adult guys photographed shirtless in a field of bluebonnets! So from the moment I heard of the rumored existence of such a photo featuring Rick Perry, I was determined to find it.

Many politicos told me about the photo. Supposedly it had Perry and Former Legislator, together, in a field of bluebonnets—with their shirts off! Absolutely conclusive, irrefutable proof. Well, maybe not, but a really cool piece of evidence to find.

The story I heard the most was that a well-known Democrat, "Former Officeholder," had claimed far and wide to have a copy of the photo during one of his campaigns. Other former officeholders independently told me about his claim.

One day I learned that Former Officeholder was scheduled to speak at a public breakfast gathering in Austin.

That was a problem for me. I'm basically nocturnal. I don't eat breakfast, at least not before 3:00 pm, and I generally believe that exposure to pre-noon light is unhealthy.

But I had to get my hands on the famous bluebonnets photo. So I dragged myself out of bed early that morning and went to the event. Sure enough, when I arrived, Former Officeholder was working the room chatting up the audience. I waited until Former Officeholder finished the conversation and then I walked up to him, deliberately standing as close as I could to invade his personal space.

He greeted me and I immediately asked, "So, Former Officeholder, do you still have a copy of that photo you have of Rick Perry and Former Legislator sitting in a field of Texas bluebonnets?"

Former Officeholder seemed stunned. In slow motion his face scrunched up like a prune. He looked at the ceiling. Finally, he said, "Glen, I have no idea what you're talking about."

I asked a second time, slowly, "You know, the picture of Rick Perry and Former Legislator sitting in a field of Texas bluebonnets."

"Uh, I really don't know what you are talking about," he said again, apparently in some pain.

"Sure you do. Remember? When you were running for [a particular office], you gay-baited all over Texas. Told hundreds of people Perry was a homosexual and you had a picture of him and Former Legislator sitting in a field of Texas Bluebonnets. Many people have told me about that. Do you still have it?"

Former Officeholder pruned up again. He looked like he was shitting in his pants. Another long pause. "I think I heard about it from [Political Consultant X]. Well, I don't remember it's a field of bluebonnets. I think it's just them standing without their shirts with something in their hands … hoes or something." More pruning.

"Hoes?" I asked. "You mean hoes like this?"—I gestured as if chopping the ground. "Or hoes like—?" I gestured somewhat obscenely, as if stroking something else.

"It's all just ancient history! Ancient history!" He abruptly turned his back to me and quickly walked away.

So there was a photo! I had not mentioned the subjects were shirtless but that's how he described the men in it.

At that moment, another coincidence: I looked out into the audience and immediately spotted "Political Consultant X." I walked over to him and asked, "Hey, I was just talking to Former Officeholder, and he said that you had told him about a photo you had of Rick Perry and Former Legislator sitting in a field of bluebonnets with their shirts off. Do you have that?"

"Hell no," he said, "if I had that photo, I would have used it in campaigns against Perry 20 years ago!"

I'm convinced that the photo exists, or once did. But I never did find a copy.

James

By this time I'd sent hundreds of emails to my contacts and to potential sources, and word was getting out about my investigation. Reporters started calling, trying to see if I was on to anything concrete. Meanwhile, The Journalist had been working on sources close to Joey the Hustler, looking for confirmation and trying to get Joey to talk with him directly again. The Journalist said that to run the story, we'd need to focus on the three strongest individuals with information about Perry, and that one of the men would need to be on the record. The Journalist planned to focus on Geoff Connor, Joey the Hustler, and the Former Legislator, when something ... juicier... came up.

A friend, "Prominent Lawer," replied to one of my fishing email inquiries and said he had a friend—I'll call him "James"—who told him a story about being picked up by Perry on the jogging trail. The story was consistent with what I had heard in the stories about Perry cruising guys in his running shorts at the water station.

EMAIL 6/30/2011 12:54 PM From Prominent Lawyer

I talked with a guy in real estate who had sex with Perry (Perry was top, small penis, took condom with him so there would be no DNA evidence). Perry picked him up on jogging trail and went back to his house. DPS stood watch outside, ironically.

He won't come forth because he said it's his word against Perry (and, I suspect, fears repercussion on his business)

If we could get James the Jogger to talk on the record, that would be a real silver bullet to back up our other stories told second-hand by people whose friends claimed to have had same-sex encounters with Perry.

The Journalist got James's contact information from the attorney and called him.

EMAIL 7/11/2011 6:28 PM From The Journalist

Subject: hey

Glen:

Just talked to the jogger. He said he had many hookups. But did not recall hooking up with Perry. He was pissed that I called. He hung up. I called back and he just wouldn't talk.

EMAIL 7/11/2011 6:23 PM To The Journalist

well that sucks (and not in a good way).

Guess he thought the troopers were just hot gay guys dressing up in uniforms for the fun of it outside his door.

EMAIL 7/11/2011 6:40 PM From The Journalist

Didn't even get that far. That's why I called back. To mention the troopers. I think he was really pissed. I think he fucked Perry. But there's nothing I can do unless you can think of a new strategy. Any ideas?

When I talked to The Journalist on the phone the next day, he said that the guy had said "I've fucked a lot of guys. Don't remember fucking Rick

Perry." Then The Journalist realized he had called the wrong number! My response was, "Well, that's Austin liberals for you. You call a guy and he just jokes with you about fucking a lot of guys." We laughed a lot about this mistaken lead.

<u>Department of Perry Secrets?</u>

While The Journalist continued trying to connect with the real James, something about Perry's running man encounter jogged my memory. I recalled my conversations with Charles Soechting, the former TDP chair, who himself was a former Department of Public Safety officer. I'd often suspected that Soechting's rumors were from the DPS officers assigned to protect Perry 24-7.

As Governor, Perry doesn't take a step without a DPS escort alongside. On the jogging trail, there are always DPS officers on bikes a few steps behind him. If he was slipping out for anonymous sexual encounters, I figured DPS would have to know. They were also assigned to the Governor's mansion, standing guard in a carriage house in the rear where both the family and household staff would enter and exit the house. If we could find a DPS officer or two willing to spill the beans, we might get interesting stories. We also might learn more about Anita and the Geoff Connor story as well.

DPS officers are very well-trained at their jobs and take them very seriously. My friends who worked in the Ann Richards administration tell a story of a time the late Governor tried to escape her DPS detail by slipping out the back door. They caught Ann in an alley. Later, a supervisor chastised Ann for trying to get away: "Did you want to cost those nice officers their jobs?" Living with constant law enforcement supervision was simply part of the job of being Governor.

EMAIL 7/15/2011 4:19 PM To The Journalist

I'm curious if the Governor can use DPS as an alibi. For example, if a person said that the Governor came over to their house for beer and good "conversation." Could the Governor use the DPS to cover his ass and say

"No, The Governor has never been to that house."
In other words, WE cannot use the DPS to know where he goes.

But can he use the DPS to disprove where he goes?

You following my drift?

Call me if this isn't clear what I'm asking.

I started digging again. An elected official told me a story she'd read on a blog about a DPS trooper who was suspended for watching porn on his cruiser in-car video monitor and who, according to the blogger, went public in retaliation with a claim that he had driven Perry to his various homosexual hookups.

Another friend told me about a DPS officer who had transferred from the Governor's detail. My friend thought that was odd, because trailing the Governor around had to be a pretty cushy job. The officer told my friend that "it got to be too much." My friend thought the officer meant the hours and time away from his family.

But the officer clarified: "No, I mean it just got too weird. The personal stuff."

My friend understood him to mean that the officer was referring to Perry's sexcapades. I got a name and address for the DPS officer. DPS officers have confidentiality restrictions, and I was reluctant to encourage the man to risk his pension for telling us what he knew.

July Heat, Barton Springs

Suddenly, it was the end of July, the height of an oppressive summer in the middle of a record-setting drought. Temperatures rarely dipped below 100 degrees. Back in the spring, Rick Perry had taken to "praying for rain" to end the drought. Mother Nature laughed, rain avoided Austin.

Our investigation into Perry's sexual proclivities was also running hot. The Journalist came to Austin to put the final touches on his story. I was certain that we'd be able to get on-the-record sources for our three strongest stories and prove the truth of Perry's alleged homosexual relationships. At that point, I thought that if The Journalist ran his story, it would probably end Perry's presidential campaign.

As I looked back at this point, it was hard to believe that all of these stories about Perry had come out in just one month since The Journalist first called me to ask what I knew. I was excited to finally meet The Journalist. I was even more excited for the meeting The Journalist had set up with James the Jogger. The burden of proof and threat of lawsuits had loomed over our entire investigation. The Journalist needed these men to look him in the eye and state unequivocally–and, ideally, on the record– that they'd had sex with Rick Perry. If that was the truth, The Journalist needed the evidence.

I told The Journalist to make some time for the high points of Austin in the summer: a Barton Springs swim, Tex Mex lunches, and the steak dinner he'd promised me for helping with all of his on-the-ground in-the-bars research in Austin.

And I didn't even realize yet that we would soon take an important field trip to visit the one man repeatedly identified in reported rumors as supposedly having had a real relationship with Perry, and was his most commonly mentioned alleged paramour: Geoff Connor.

What Is "Gay"?

Now, for those of you that just picked up this book to get your jollies reading about Perry's sexual adventures, I need you to indulge me for a moment. Throughout this story, I've been careful to refer to Perry's activities as homosexual or same-sex, never "gay." That's because as far as I'm concerned, Rick Perry isn't gay. He's a man who has sexual encounters with other men. Those men predominantly identify themselves as gay. But Rick Perry is not, as far as I am concerned, gay.

Being gay is much more than just sex. Being gay is having an emotional relationship with a member of the same sex.

Several of the GLBT activists I talked to about my research, and some of the men who admitted tricking with Perry, were worried that if the story got out, Perry would be identified as "gay" in a way that would denigrate the entire community. The accusation that Perry is gay would be perceived as wrong or immoral, thus associating the gayness itself–rather than Perry's hypocrisy and use of his office to hide his sexual activities– with something bad. That's harmful to the entire GLBT cause. There's nothing wrong with being gay or straight or bisexual or anything that any number of consenting adults do together. Most people I know don't care who the Governor has sex with. What they do care about is hypocrisy in public leaders. What they do care about is the hypocrisy surrounding GLBT issues that Perry has exhibited in the last six years of his governorship and the increasing hypocrisy evident in his presidential campaign. Given all of the reports and stories I've heard during the last few months, Perry's attacks on same-sex relationships appear to be astonishing, head-snapping hypocrisy.

During my time as the lobbyist for the Lesbian/Gay Rights Lobby of Texas, I interacted with Perry—mostly in social circumstances, rather than in legislative settings. He was a bad vote on gay issues and HIV issues, and nothing I could do would change that. However, he was what I'd call a "harmless" bad vote. He'd never authored an anti-gay bill or amendment, nor did he take to the microphone during floor debate to bash the queers.

Throughout his time as a State Representative, and then as Texas Agriculture Commissioner and Lt. Governor, Rick Perry was never seen as particularly anti-gay. I cannot remember a speech, a statement, or a piece of legislation he pushed that would have been of concern to GLBT Texans. In Texas, that was not a bad record for my issues and constituents.

In the 1999 Legislative Session, Governor Bush pushed a minority in the Senate to use a parliamentary procedure to keep the James Byrd Hate Crimes Act from finally passing. Although Lieutenant Governor Rick Perry presided over the State Senate, he didn't play a public role in killing the bill. The Legislature finally passed it after Bush was elected President. Governor Perry signed the bill. He did make one request: that the representatives of the Lesbian/Gay Right Lobby and the openly gay state Representative Glen Maxey not be present at the bill signing ceremony. For me, it was a small price to pay for his signature on this important advance.

Perry's jerk rightward on GLBT issues was first spotlighted at the close of the 2005 legislative session. George W. Bush had just been re-elected President, in large part due to inflaming anti-gay sentiment among conservative church-goers in swing states. During the session, Texas Republican leaders joined the ranks of states trying to constitutionally ban gays and lesbians from marrying. They put a state constitutional amendment against marriage equality on the November 2005 ballot.

After Texas passed the amendment, Perry held a huge, symbolic "bill signing" ceremony. It was at a private Christian school in Fort Worth. But it was a charade. Texas Governors don't sign constitutional amendments. But there Perry was, surrounded by right-wing fundamentalists and evangelical Christians as he signed a document for the cameras. Now, for six years, we've watched Rick Perry lurch, jump, and dance to the farthest extremes of the right wing. In August 2011 Perry organized a full-fledged prayer palooza, "The Response," in Houston, with America's most virulent anti-gay religious bigots joining religious-right-Rick on stage.

In effect, Perry has renounced his previous reasonableness shown in signing the Texas hate-crimes legislation. In my view, based on what I've learned, that's pure hypocrisy and pure opportunism. If Rick Perry has had homosexual encounters, that's not the problem. The problem is his astonishing hypocrisy on GLBT issues—perhaps most recently best exhibited by his December 2011 TV ad, entitled "Strong." In the ad, he suggests that it's wrong to let gays and lesbians serve openly in the military.

I will state this to my dying breath or until and unless he declares himself otherwise–Rick Perry is NOT gay. For decades GLBT activists have worked to educate the nation that we're just like everyone else in our lives, loves, and relationships.

My investigation has identified substantial evidence indicating that Rick Perry has participated in homosexual sex acts. Random or planned, anonymous or with an acquaintance, such sex acts are not what "gay" means in today's society. If Rick Perry has had homosexual encounters, I doubt that he has had emotional relationships with members of the same sex. If that's true, he's not gay, as we define the term. Those relationships would not mean that he's gay—they would just mean that he likes to have sex with men. That's a critically important distinction.

Field Trip To Bastrop

After resigning from his office as Secretary of State, Geoff Connor seems to have tried to lead a relatively private life, focused on his work as a mediator and attorney. We heard from a mutual friend that he'd moved out to Bastrop, just east of Austin. He purchased a historic house to fix up.

The Journalist and I decided to drive out to Bastrop to ask Connor about his relationship with Perry. The Journalist had talked to Connor twice before, once on tape. Now it was time to confront him in person.

We pulled up to an imposing two-story historic house with round, pointed turrets and two Texas State Historical Markers, perched on the banks of the Colorado River.

The Journalist parked the rental car directly in front of the house, right by the walkway to the front porch.

"Don't stop! Pull up further," I demanded.

"Why?"

"Pull up further until I tell you to stop."

When I finally told him it was safe to stop the car, The Journalist asked why this spot was better than directly in front of Connor's house.

"You see that big oak tree right there? It's now between where I'm sitting and the front door. You might not know this, but in Texas gays have guns too. You might get shot, but I'm cowering right here behind this tree in this car."

The Journalist walked to Connor's door. Connor appeared and The Journalist asked him to refute the story about Perry. Connor's response was the same as the preceding two phone conversations, essentially stating, "I'm no longer a public official and I don't care to comment on that. I suggest you ask Rick Perry."

After Connor stated his non-denial, he asked The Journalist to leave and slammed the door. The Journalist walked around the front yard taking pictures. I told him to leave before he got arrested for trespassing.

"I'm not afraid of getting arrested," The Journalist barked.

My response was more on point.

"It's 110 degrees right now. I assure you the Bastrop jail is not air conditioned. I shall not die of heat stroke in there. Let's get the hell outta here!"

Texas law also grants broad protection for the use of force against trespassers.

On our drive back, we reflected that it was odd that Connor never stated a direct denial. It wasn't the unequivocal denial Perry might have wanted from his purported former lover. To my knowledge, no one had gotten Connor on the record in 2004 when the story broke. Connor's odd non-denial certainly felt prepared, as if Connor had been waiting for this to happen since Perry's presidential run breathed new life into the old rumors. Why didn't Connor just say "No, I never had homosexual relations with Perry"? If that was true, why didn't Connor say that? That seems so simple. What Connor said seemed so much more provocative.

Gay Bars and Gay Downsizing

Our Perry field trips continued after dark. The Journalist and I spent some time talking with bartenders at the oldest gay bar in Austin. I'd made the rounds early on to ask old-timers and regulars who'd been around the scene since the 1980s if they'd ever heard anything.

A gay bar bartender or barfly can be either an excellent gossip or a safety deposit box for secrets. My early inquiries at Oil Can Harry's, in Austin's famous warehouse district, came up dry. Though GLBT community friends repeatedly told me that their old-timer bartender knew stories about Perry, he ignored my request that he call The Journalist. He even ignored my notes with attached $10 bills, asking him to call me. When I finally talked to him in person, he didn't even acknowledge the inquiry.

I had much better luck at Rain, another downtown Austin fixture. The bartender was a former legislative aide to a west Texas Legislator and boyfriend of one of my former interns. We had a great conversation, amidst loud music, half-naked boys, and yelling customers. In between drunks and dick dancers, I learned that the bartender had heard lots of Perry rumors and did know a Hustler named Joey. He agreed to ask other bartenders as well.

But we hit the jackpot at Charlie's Bar, the now-shuttered gay watering hole, just two blocks from the Capitol. Charlie's had been around for almost three decades. It was a favored happy hour destination for professional gay men. During the daytime it wasn't an aggressive meat-market like the nightclubs downtown, but rather a destination for gays in search of drinks and gossip, and also had a popular weekly steak dinner night.

The Journalist and I camped out at Charlie's one night and quickly befriended the bartender. He's heard the Perry stories for years. To impress upon our out-of-town Journalist friend the ubiquity of the rumors, the bartender said he would ask the next ten patrons if they'd ever heard stories about Rick Perry having sex with other men. All ten said yes. Even I was amazed.

The bartender followed up each affirmative answer with, "Why do you think that?" Most cited the Connor story. But one patron had a new tale.

"I was at a party with him back in the '80s in Lost Creek," the patron said. Lost Creek is a very chi-chi neighborhood in West Austin, very exclusive.

I asked the patron, "What makes you think it was a gay party?"

"Well, it wasn't a 'check your clothes at the door' gay party. But everyone was gay." The patron started listing the host and other guests as I raced to scribble the names on a cocktail napkin.

"Whoa, don't be writing this down!" protested the patron. The Journalist explained who he was and the nature of our investigation into proving the Perry rumors, publishing them in a national news source and exposing a hypocrite. The patron agreed to go on the record, and The Journalist's tape recorder clicked on. He retold his story to The Journalist.

At one point I asked, "Why do you think Perry is gay, just because he was at a gay party?"

"Well honey, he came in with a guy who had his pinkie finger hooked into his belt loop and it never came out of there all night long." In Texas, pinkie-finger hooking is pretty flagrant.

I'd heard other people trading rumors about Perry at a gay party. The Journalist and I compiled a list of attendees from the bar patron. We contacted several, but no one could recall Perry being in attendance. I wasn't surprised. At the time of the party in the 1980s, Perry was a harmless newbie legislator. There was no reason any of the other guests should or would have recognized the bottom-rung politician from out of town.

The bartender himself had another story that would prove fruitful, however. Due to its proximity to the Capitol, Charlie's was a favored destination of the gay men in state government. Three young men working in the governor's office came in to drink frequently. One night, a member of that group came in looking like he was ready to punch a hole through the wall, according to a second bartender in a later conversation. It was just after the Geoff Connor speculation hit the papers.

The young man apparently said, "I'm a Republican, and I got organized out of a job because the Governor got a blow job!" He explained to the bartender that as part of the fall-out or cover-up, the young man and his two gay colleagues had apparently been fired in a purge of all gay or seemingly-gay staffers. As another bartender phrased it, somewhat more colorfully, "after the governor got busted for sucking dick in the mansion, they all got fired." The gay staffer was angry that his career had been derailed by what he saw as the effort to sweep the Connor incident under the rug.

We asked the bartender if he could recall the names of the three gay guys who were fired. After looking through his Facebook friends on his phone, he produced the name of the first, "Robby," who ironically also had been a bartender at the bar. He was sure the second was "Pete." The third he could only recall as being a Hispanic man.

FACEBOOK MESSAGE 7/26/2011 3:22 PM To Robby

Glen Maxey:

Hey [Robby]:
Just checking to see if you used to bartend at Charlie's? and once interned for Governor Perry?

Can I give you a call? Is there a good number to reach you? or can you call me?

Need to ask you about some Perry stuff from years ago... totally off the record.

Glen Maxey

Robby simply replied "Yes" and added his number. I thought I should call a Facebook friend of his first for more background. I made an error in the call though. I absent-mindedly thought I was calling the friend of Robby's, but dialed Robby's number instead. I took notes on my computer as we talked. I think this conversation is almost verbatim:

"Hi, my name is Glen. I'm the former gay legislator. I'm working on a story with a reporter about Governor Perry. We heard from a bartender that you might know the names of some guys who worked for the Governor and got fired right after the rumors about Perry being gay hit the paper."

"I signed a confidentiality agreement. I can't talk. I'm really sorry."

Wait a second. I realized my mistake – I had accidentally called one of the fired gay guys! I immediately changed my strategy.

"OK... Wow... Were you one of them?"

"I can't say. I'm really sorry. I'm sorry."

His voice quivered. There was a long pause.

"Well, Robby, can you tell me if we're onto something here?

"Ahhhh... ahhhh...."

I could hear the deliberation and tension in his voice as he stalled. He seemed to want to talk but to fear the possible consequences of violating the confidentiality agreement he had signed with the Governor's office.

"Yes. Can't tell you. I can't tell you anything more. I'm sorry."

Fuck.

"Well, thanks for sharing, Robby. I know this is a difficult topic. Let me know if there is anything you can share."

"OK. I'm sorry. Goodbye."

Robby wasn't going to talk to us, but given his non-denial and hints that we were on the right track, I was determined to track down his two other colleagues who were ousted from the Governor's office. I also needed to find out what their official positions were.

Meanwhile I reached out through Facebook to another young man, "Pete," who the bartender had also mentioned by name. I spent hours sending emails to Pete and Pete's Facebook friends. I went through dozens of Lexis/Nexis addresses for men named Pete with the same last name. The Journalist and I even made a twenty mile drive to the suburbs to knock on the door of the most likely one. It was exhausting. I even emailed a woman I thought was Pete's mother, who I found on Facebook. I asked if her son ever worked for the Governor. She wrote me a very nice reply, but said it wasn't her son. Our search was fruitless.

But then out of the blue Pete responded to my Facebook message. His only response was that he "knew the Governor through his charities," whatever the hell that meant.

Pete had an understandable reason not to dredge up old memories, if he had any—he said his partner had just died and he was sick. I didn't pursue the matter with him.

All I knew about the third man was that he was Hispanic. Without a name, it was a dead end.

Jogging Through Craigslist

The Journalist was able to connect with James the Jogger, who claimed he had been picked up by Perry while out for a run. They set up a meeting while The Journalist was here in Austin.

EMAIL 7/21/2011 1:07 PM From The Journalist

So not only do we have to convince [James] to tell his complete story. But we have to try very hard to get him to go on the record. Same with [Joey] and [Former Legislator.] At some point, we need to get tough and just make the case to these guys. I've written 1,000 words so far. I see the story being roughly 2500 words. The thing that jumps out: the jogger could and should be on the record. If he can't, he's got to give us someone else he told the story to.

The Journalist had purposefully not gone into details until he could do so face-to-face. The appointment was set as soon as The Journalist hit the ground in Austin. He went directly from the airport to interview him.

I was beside myself to get a report about the encounter. Several hours after the meeting was supposed to have begun, I couldn't resist texting The Journalist to see what was going on.

TEXT 7/25/2011 To The Journalist

Glen Maxey: Either it is going really well or you're in a ditch somewhere?

The Reporter called me soon afterward and repeated to me the story he'd just heard from James. It turned out that the story James told in person was far different from the story we'd heard from his attorney friend.

According to James, Perry hadn't actually picked him up on the running trail. James said he encountered Perry by responding to a Craigslist post from a man looking for an anonymous sexual encounter!

James had evidently been unwilling to share this sordid detail with his attorney friend. The posting asked for someone willing to unlock the door, turn off the lights, and lie face-down on the bed, legs spread. James replied to the ad, and did as instructed. As he lay on his bed in the dark, James heard someone struggling to open the door. Shielding his eyes, he ran out and opened the door. James went back into the room, followed by the mystery man, who proceeded to look behind mirrors and picture frames and in light fixtures, as if checking for cameras or recording devices. The man in his bedroom was average build, wearing running clothes, a baseball cap pulled low over his face.

Apparently satisfied with his room inspection, the guest went to the business at hand.

Here is James's account of what happened, as The Journalist retold it to me:

"He jerked down his shorts. It lasted about a minute. He had a little dick. It was the worst fuck of my life. And on top of it all he stunk because he had been jogging. He then pulled up his shorts and put the used condom in his pocket."

As the mystery man tried to leave James's apartment, he struggled with the front door, which had a tendency to jam. The man started yelling for James to help him. James got up to open the door.

As James opened it, two things happened. First, as the man walked out, his face was illuminated, and seen by James for the first time.

"Oh my God," thought James, "I just got fucked by Rick Perry!"

Second, as Perry started sprinting toward a black SUV in the driveway, James saw another person also in jogging clothes and cap moving quickly toward them, weapon drawn—apparently alerted and concerned by Perry's noise as he wrestled with the front door. The gunman retreated when he saw that Perry was okay and headed back to the car. James went back inside, astonished by the remarkable events.

It seemed obvious to me and to The Journalist that DPS had brought Perry to the hookup and took him home afterward.

I was giddy when The Journalist told me James's story. This was the best witness yet—not just an actual sex partner, but one arranged via an anonymous Craigslist encounter! At that point, I felt sure we had a story that The Journalist would have no difficulty publishing.

But The Journalist was skeptical. "Who posts a Craigslist ad like that?" he asked. "Face down, assume the position?" I explained that it was not that unusual. The ad that James described was pretty typical for a married or closeted man who wanted sex and didn't want to be identified. I'd seen many such ads in my own perusals of the m4m section. Usually, though, the person on the receiving end, so to speak, expected something in return. And given what I knew about Perry's general attitudes and political practices, it was no surprise to me that Perry wasn't inclined to be generous toward the Texans he was fucking.

But why would Perry take a risk on anonymous encounters? Another journalist I talked to later had covered similar high-profile politician sexual escapades. He gave me the explanation that seemed to make the most sense. Some politicians, he said, have personalities with giant egos coupled with a sense of arrogant invulnerability. "I'm so great, I'm so smart—they'll never catch me!" Bill Clinton, John Edwards, John Ensign, Gary Hart, Herman Cain, Larry Craig, Mark Foley, Newt Gingrich—the list goes on and on. It's not one political party. And I'm sure the psychology is more complex and varied than the reporter's simplistic explanation takes into account. But it sort of makes sense. In any event, we see the same pattern repeated so often.

And consider where Rick Perry lives—in Austin. Although Austin has a large gay population and is famously tolerant, it is overwhelmingly Democratic—at the same time that state government is controlled completely by Republicans. Lots of gay Republican government staffers frequent gay bars in a fairly public manner. But Rick Perry couldn't do that. If he has these proclivities, his options are limited. Anonymous sex, in the dark, with an armed guard outside—by comparison, that's not so risky.

I also explained to The Journalist that I wasn't surprised by the discrepancy between what James told his attorney friend and what he told The Journalist. James was understandably reluctant to tell his lawyer friend that he used the "Casual Encounters" section on Craigslist for some fun. In reality, Craigslist and other Internet sites have replaced the more lurid bathhouses and parks that men used to cruise in past decades for quick, anonymous encounters. Unfortunately, we couldn't find the Craigslist posting–they are deleted after thirty days.

Once The Journalist concluded that James's story was pretty solid, he was sure that he could convince James to go on the record, or at least give us a friend who would go on the record to retell the story. Before leaving his interview, The Journalist got a list of friends and roommates to whom James told the story at the time, who he in turn would call to corroborate.

That night, The Journalist and I ate a celebratory steak dinner. I was confident we had enough to expose the truth about Perry. I couldn't remember the last time an expensive piece of meat tasted so good.

Loose Ends and New Leads

The closer we got to the end of the investigation, the more the loose ends seemed to tie themselves together.

While The Journalist was in Austin, another of my fishing expedition emails bore fruit. One friend responded that he and his partner knew a guy who had told a story of being "hit on" on the jogging trail. The couple had emailed the fellow to see if he would tell his story to The Journalist. We were impatient. We went to their home to see if they would reveal the guy's name so that The Journalist could interview him before The Journalist left Austin the next day. They hesitated, but we learned his name was "BJ" and that he worked at one of the largest upscale food stores in town.

Days went by, The Journalist flew home, and BJ's friends hadn't heard back from him about whether or not he'd be interviewed. I decided to go to the store myself to try to find this additional lead. You might wonder how I could hope to find this potential lead in a large store ("Excuse me, Cute Service-Desk Boy, could you point me to the department where I'm most likely to find someone who had a hookup with Governor Rick Perry—would that be in meat or produce?"). I thought it might not be difficult—I had his name, BJ. And I am rather experienced at finding gay men.

EMAIL 8/2/2011 3:04 pm to The Journalist

Well, the prices there are too fucking high. I did buy a loaf of bread and some water. All I could afford. LOL

There is no BJ that the service desk peeps know.

There were two very nice gay boys at the counter where you order your personal shopper to get shit for you. One thought there was BJ in the meet dept., but I had just asked the oldest employee in there if he knew a BJ...nada

I asked about 20 people in different departments and none knew him. The cute gay boys (above) said they knew everyone on the floor and didn't know a BJ. But they said there were another 200 people in the "food prep" department and they didn't know those folks.... plus the corporate folks upstairs.

EMAIL 8/2/2011 3:05 To The Journalist

sorry, that was meat dept... not meet department. I think the gay boys were the "meet dept"

EMAIL 8/2/2011 3:09 From The Journalist

ugh. only hope is that your friend gets back to you on which department. Maybe there is a "meet dept."

A few weeks later, after The Journalist got back to D.C., BJ got in touch with him and told his story about the encounter with Perry on the jogging trail. BJ was as adamant that the interaction between him and Perry on the trail was a sexual advance—and equally adamant that he didn't take Perry up on the offer. The jogger also told The Journalist of a friend who supposedly hooked up with Perry through a Craigslist ad. The Craigslist encounter stories matched up—it looks like BJ and James were friends. Small world.

Meanwhile, new leads kept coming in from unexpected sources. A typical example: I sent a Facebook birthday greeting to a young gay graphic artist friend who had moved to New York City a few years earlier. In our chat session catching up, I told him I was researching about Rick Perry's possible homosexual hookups. He immediately replied that he had a friend who was a member of the Republican National Committee from New Jersey. This RNC member was a closeted gay Republican. He had told a story of Rick Perry at a New York fundraiser where Perry supposedly "hit on" a NYC police officer working security and had disappeared with said officer during the event. Once again, "everyone knew" they had hooked up. Apparently the story had spread widely in the New York area.

Prime Source

What became clear to me throughout the investigation was that Joey was a prime source. I felt that we needed to land him on the record and give him the opportunity to control his own story. I also was concerned that if this story broke, it could radically transform Joey's lifestyle. I wanted him to tell his story, but I wanted him to take reasonable steps to protect himself in case Perry or his fellow travelers attacked him viciously and publicly.

I also came to realize that despite Joey's highly experienced sex life, he seemed naïve and innocent in some of the ways of the world. He described himself as being apolitical, but in reality, Joey was politically clueless. He didn't understand why anyone would care about the dirt he had on the Governor, and had no idea how much someone might pay to expose the story. Joey didn't even know that Perry was potentially running for President! His lack of political savvy was quite possibly the biggest obstacle to getting his story on the record.

TEXT 8/6/2011 6:34 pm To Joey the Hustler

Glen Maxey: [Joey.] What do you need to confirm the story you've told people over the years about being hired for parties where Rick Perry was? How much?

Joey the Hustler: What would the party speaking to me value it at if it were true…

Glen Maxey: Well there are lots of folks I know who would pay. But they would need some solid info.

Glen Maxey: Cuz if there is, I'll sure as hell be the go between.

Joey the Hustler: That would be a good idea. There is fire. The question is what would be solid I don't have DNA or the like.

Glen Maxey: Can you name anyone else who was involved?

Glen Maxey: I promise I won't fuck you over.

Joey the Hustler: definitely a possibility.

Glen Maxey: Ok. Let me talk to some folks and see how to proceed.

Glen Maxey: Never done this kind of transaction. So need to check how to do this to protect you.

Glen Maxey: Give me til early next week. OK?

Glen Maxey: I was the openly gay state legislator. Glen Maxey. I'm legitimate. Google me.

Joey the Hustler: Take all the time that you need I am not in a hurry.

Glen Maxey: Cool.

Joey the Hustler: I have done more then Googled.

Glen Maxey: What's that mean?

Joey the Hustler: Everyone knows everyone some how.

Glen Maxey: That's very true.

Glen Maxey: Talk to you later.

It sounded like Joey had done some research of his own. Or perhaps my asking around about a hustler named Joey in every gay bar in Austin had gotten back to him and he did a little investigation concerning the person who was doing all the digging.

I didn't actually know if anyone would pay Joey for his story. But I'd read a little about such things, and I thought that if he was potentially going to experience life changing disruptions, and perhaps become embroiled in a high-publicity storm, he should prepare himself, psychologically and financially.

I found it endearing that Joey was as troubled by the burden of proof that The Journalist and I were. His comment that he hadn't saved any DNA suggested to me that he knew that people might not be inclined to believe his story.

Joey would never have come forward on his own. He'd only talked about it with his friends and his regular circle of gay contacts. Joey was in no rush to tell his story—he didn't understand the urgency of it, even though Rick Perry was probably going to announce his Presidential campaign within two weeks.

The Journalist was working to finalize the story. His last hurdle seemed to be getting James to use his name on the record. The publisher wasn't going to allow including the Craigslist encounter without it. Also, fact checkers had to verify every other on-the-record statement, which could take some time. I was getting agitated and impatient. I had started working on the story on June 23rd and here we were some seven weeks later—and still no story.

EMAIL 8/12/2011 11:08 PM From The Journalist

As of now, I have more than 20 people in the story that are on the record. Some will drop out. But some of the new editions really make the story stronger and more powerful. I have one more lead I'm tracking down. And just waiting on [James.] He's willing to use a variation of his first name. Trying to get him to use his last name. Sent him the story. Fingers crossed.

As I discussed and debated the possible story with my friends in Austin the contrarian view on timing was that it would have more impact if we could wait until Perry sewed up the Republican nomination. We thought he had an excellent shot—he had never lost a race in Texas, was an excellent fundraiser, and he had worked very hard for and earned substantial Tea Party and conservative Christian support, and those groups seemed to have seized control of the Republican nominating process. Much of the Republican base seemed to want anyone but Romney, and Perry seemed to be perfectly positioned to present the "true conservative" alternative option.

Thus, the thinking of this group of my friends was that if the story was not published until after Perry got the nomination, the negative effect would likely be maximized.

But I didn't want to wait, and more importantly, neither did The Journalist. I also knew that in any event, I had no control over the timing of publication. Moreover, while we politicos say that politics is all about timing, we also know that predicting the course of a presidential race in the middle of a contested primary campaign is next to impossible. The chips just needed to fall however they fell and whenever they fell.

I felt pretty sure that the Journalists and I were the only people who'd tracked down Joey and James and gotten their stories corroborated, I heard about other reporters continuing to nose around some of the same rumors. The Journalist and his publisher knew that, too, and they didn't want to get scooped.

But at that point, I was confident that everything was coming together. Publication and exposure of Perry's secret sexcapades seemed inevitable and imminent.

Another piece fell into place: thankfully, James agreed to be identified by his first initial and last name—and it was a common enough name that he'd still have some measure of privacy. We hoped that would satisfy the publisher on the James angle.

On August 12, The Journalist submitted his story for final approval. The very next day, Rick Perry announced that he was running for President of the United States. The timing was perfect, and publication seemed assured. But our story doesn't end so easily, not yet...

Part III: Burden of Proof

Two days later, The Journalist was still waiting to hear from his editors.

I didn't like the delay. I was ready for the story to run. I'd spent two months of my life doing nothing but poking into Perry's private life and was ready to see results.

In preparation for what I assumed might be a media circus, I'd laid in provisions, put double locks on my door, and done my laundry. While my friends wanted to throw a party when the story came out, I knew I'd just want to hide in a bunker until it blew over.

Already since Perry's announcement I'd started receiving press calls from every GLBT publication in the country. Most were just looking into Perry's record on gay issues, but a few sniffed around the rumors. When the story broke, there would be a frenzy of reporters, tabloids, and bloggers in Austin, trying to find other tricks and prove or disprove the stories.

While I felt good about having succeeded where so many investigators failed, I was frustrated that The Journalist's publishers and parent company were taking their sweet-ass time getting the story out.

The Chief Editor at National News Outlet asked The Journalist to add elements about how Austin's vibe let these secrets stay mostly buried. But frankly, it wasn't our laid back, libertine attitude that let Perry escape exposure.

Perry is very powerful in Texas. After his ten years as Governor, he and his inner circle of advisors and lobbyist cronies have been able to appoint every state agency head, university regent, and important administrator in the Texas. His stranglehold on the state is such that if you cross him or one of his pals, you could expect professional, public, or private retaliation.

Many of those who knew intimate details are involved in politics or work for the state and feared retribution if they came forward. Few normal people want to be thrust into that kind of spotlight, where national scrutiny could turn every element of your life upside down and inside out. Furthermore, many people with stories to tell are either closeted or formerly in the closet, or knew about Perry through their own connections to the sex trade. After all, if someone like James the Jogger fibbed to his own friend about how he met Perry, why would he want to tell the entire world that he picked up men for anonymous sex via the Internet?

But it's more than just power that helped protect Perry. Back when he was leading a less secretive life–when he was a young legislator and I was hearing about Perry from the boys in the bars–he had little reason to try so hard to hide. Most people probably couldn't pick their state legislator out of a line-up, let alone one from Haskell County. Most Texans couldn't find Haskell County on a map. What impetus would anyone have had at the time to out him, if they even recognized who he was?

The Rolling Stone

EMAIL 8/15/2011 3:31 PM *From The Journalist*

Glen: Have you heard footsteps from Rolling Stone mag on this story?

That was curious. I replied that no, I hadn't heard of anyone from *Rolling Stone* poking around. Usually if anyone was working on the gay rumors, they'd call the first and only open gay legislator in Texas, yours truly.

EMAIL 8/15/2011 6:06 PM *From The Journalist*

Can you email me again your exchange with [Joey?]

EMAIL 8/16/2011 10:28 AM *From The Journalist*

Want to ask you if there's anyone else--now that he's running for prez--we could go back to?

EMAIL 8/16/2011 10:31 AM *To The Journalist*

I'm cogitating on that question. Meaning people we passed or who wouldn't talk before??

EMAIL 8/16/2011 10:26 AM *From The Journalist*

People who wouldn't talk before. Also: who do you think would step up if the media came calling? Who would defend this piece? I assume that you would be happy to go on Maddow or something. But who else? It's an argument I'm going to try and use with [James.]

I made him a list of people who would defend James personally, and thought maybe I could come up with a list of public figures who would be likely to defend the entire story in public.

I was worried. I got the sense that The Journalist's publishers were starting to give him the runaround. We'd spent two months getting people on the record with what I thought were solid stories about Perry's gay connections. Now the publisher was moving the goal post?

The next day, Rasmussen released a national poll of 1000 voters with Perry in the lead, 29% to 18%, over Romney.

Now was the time!

For some reason, the Journalist decided that if he couldn't verify other parts of the stories, he could at least try to see if he could disprove them. Earlier, The Journalist had sent a series of Open Records Requests to DPS to try to shake out some details on the Governor's security detail.

Email August 05, 2011 11:38 AM From The Journalist

To: PIO - Texas DPS
Subject: interview request

Dear DPS Public Information Officer:
I am writing to request an interview with someone within DPS concerning Governor Rick Perry's security detail. I have very general questions concerning the detail. My interview would be brief. I am looking to simply find out how many officers are in his detail and if they follow him around the clock--even during Perry's jogging.

As my deadline is fast approaching, any help would be much appreciated. I can be reached via this email address. I look forward to hearing from you.

From: PIO - Texas DPS

Thank you for contacting us. We do not discuss the number of agents in the Governor's Protective Detail or specifics on his protection.

DPS refused to comment on the operations of DPS, even what kind of cars the officers drove.

The Journalist and I also kept trying to prove the stories of Robby and the other Governor's office staffers who supposedly were fired for being or seeming gay in the aftermath of the Geoff Connor incident. The Journalist filed open records requests and attempted to track down lists of all of the office's employees in the years surrounding 2004, but Robby and friends weren't listed in the documents we received. Robby wouldn't even confirm for us what his position was in the office that required him to sign a confidentiality agreement upon being fired, and his friends at the bar Charlie's couldn't remember exactly either.

But based on my long experience in Texas government, the absence of documents didn't bother me. For various reasons, document responses aren't always complete. Different agencies have different document retention-and-destruction schedules. And lots of offices, including the Governor, use interns but never turn them in on formal lists.

Rumors intensified—not those about Perry's sex life, but about our efforts to expose him.

We heard a rumor that we apparently had an affidavit from someone stating under oath that Perry had sex with men. We didn't.

The Journalist heard another story—someone told him that a friend, an artist, was an alleged former lover of Perry. The artist wasn't answering his phone, so The Journalist sent me a link to the source's Facebook profile to see if I knew him.

EMAIL 8/16/2011 4:34 PM To The Journalist

Don't know him other than seeing at events/parties. We only have 108 mutual friends...so we're not close LOL

EMAIL 8/16/2011 4:34 PM From The Journalist

HA.

EMAIL 8/16/2011 4:51 PM From The Journalist

Any chance you could see if the top 5 of those 108 mutual pals might have a home number? He's not answering at work.

EMAIL 8/16/2011 5:07 PM To The Journalist

Rolodex Glen... At your service. I'll email em.

EMAIL 8/16/2011 4:34 PM From The Journalist

Cool. Thank you. This may be the last time I ask so we should start feeling nostalgic.

Flynt Offers $1 Million

While no other publication had yet proved the rumors, as far as we knew, plenty were looking. Larry Flynt offered $1 million to anyone who could prove they'd had sex with Perry, male or female. Robert Morrow, an Austin-based Ron Paul supporter, ran a full-page ad in *The Austin Chronicle*, our alt-weekly paper, blaring "Have You Ever Had Sex With Rick Perry?" People posted the ad and the Flynt article all over Facebook.

Leads continued to flow in, some solid, some flaky. A friend of mine saw someone make an offhand comment on Facebook about someone seeing Perry at the bath houses. When my friend tracked it down, the commenter recanted and said it was just a joke, he shouldn't have posted it. Then the commenter said something unsurprising to me at this point in my investigation:

> I've heard too many stories, first hand kind of stuff, from too many people, some of whom are totally apolitical and have no agenda, not to believe.

I'd heard that over and over again.

Roller Coaster Ride

Finally, an email arrived from The Journalist that lifted my spirits.

EMAIL 8/18/2011 5:19 PM From The Journalist

Email has been sent to Perry campaign. Awaiting their response. Still do not know when the story will run or whether higher ups have signed off on it.

TELL NO ONE PLEASE.

Also, bonus: I interviewed [Famous Comedienne] about the fired staffers. She confirmed that audience members told her about it when she played Austin around the time of the controversy.

The Journalist had sent the outline of the story to the Perry campaign to give them a final chance to respond before the story ran. Surely now, finally, publication was right around the corner.

The Journalist kept checking and double checking his sources, maintaining good contact. He wanted each of those people to be ready to back up their claims—potentially to a myriad of publications and media.

Two days later, my publication roller coaster took another plunge.

EMAIL 8/20/2011 6:48 PM From The Journalist

We need to talk tomorrow. Got good news. Got bad news. Got OK news.

The Journalist's publisher was reluctant to run the story. I got the sense that lawyers above her head were concerned about potential lawsuits from the Perry team. Her main concern was apparently the reliability of Joey, our best source. His profession instantly called his whole story into question – who would believe a hustler if the Governor denied it all?

I was losing my patience. We had the story. We had what I understood to be confirmed sources. If The Journalist couldn't get his publisher to OK the story, I would just give it to someone else.

EMAIL 8/20/2011 7:16 PM To The Journalist

Ok. I'm beyond pissed about this delay.

I have a reputation in Texas and especially in the GLBT community. I've sweated bullets to find these sources for you to talk to about Perry. The longer this thing festers, the worse it will get with our sources.

I've sent over 150 emails to people ranging from bartenders to State Senators and Congressmen.

I've made dozens upon dozens of calls. I took a week to take you around to sources.

Your editors need to know that you wouldn't have the Craigs List story or the Hustler without my work and persuasion of sources to talk to you on the record.

This story needs to run. NOW. I'm looking like an idiot right now with my phone ringing off the wall with media outlets wanting to talk about Perry's sex life.

I've stonewalled them all so that you guys could do this story this past week. I have a reputation in the national media as a solid source about politics and GLBT issues in Texas. I don't intend to wreck it just so you guys can diddle around.

Right now, I have multiple requests and told them all I would call them back this week (because this story would have run, supposedly). I have the Austin American Statesman, the Houston Chronicle, The Washington Post, the Des Moines Register and RG Ratcliff's biography interview and Jim Moore and Jason Stanford's book interview. They are all set for this week.

Do what you guys have to do. Just know that if asked an honest question about what I know, Glen Maxey gives an honest answer.

Those interviews are set beginning Monday.

I went somewhat overboard in the tirade. Some of these publications had only heard rumors of the story and I had put them off. But my diatribe lit a fire under The Journalist. He wanted to know which reporters, how far along their investigations were. I joked that if he took any longer, I was going to post the whole thing on some Internet blog myself. At any rate he asked for one more day to sort this all out.

Up Again, Down Again

I received word back: The story was set to run the following Monday. That sounded great—the roller coaster had reached a high point.

And then this:

EMAIL 8/22/2011 3:17 PM From The Journalist

New twist. Perry campaign wants to meet to refute these false allegations.

EMAIL 8/22/2011 3:21 PM To The Journalist

Fuck that the campaign can refute them. Unless Perry is willing to do polygraph.

Or sit across from you...in person.

How do they know about his hookups?

I further suggest the polygraph be hooked up to his little dick

I assumed that the meeting with Perry's team would cause only more delays.

I agreed to talk to The Journalist's publisher on the phone to verify the story. My task was to make her more comfortable with our sources – a hustler, a Craigslist hookup, and their network of friends.

Then I heard that National News Outlet's publisher didn't want to talk to me after all. Instead, she proposed that they cross-break the story with other publications. They had heard that *Rolling Stone* was working on the story, too. (I suspect that was a crossed wire from when Matt Taibbi was researching his "Best Little Whore in Texas" piece, which despite the title has nothing to do with $200-an-hour hustlers, only a Governor that uses the state as his own personal slush fund.)

Meanwhile, Joey still wasn't agreeing to go on the record.

TEXT 8/23/2011 5:36 pm To Joey the Hustler

Glen Maxey: Had initial talk with my guys who want your story. It'll take a while for them to decide how to proceed

Glen Maxey: Are you in Austin on Thursday or Friday? Paying gig

Joey the Hustler: Had no plans to be

Joey the Hustler: Why?

Glen Maxey: Want to meet up.

Glen Maxey: Are u in Denton like your website says?

Joey the Hustler: Dallas really. Was looking at the students up there for a toy...

Joey the Hustler: I saw your ad in the paper.

He meant the Robert Morrow ad, the one that read "Have You Had Sex With Rick Perry?".

Glen Maxey: That was not me.

Glen Maxey: That guy was looking for his women hookups

Joey the Hustler: I am sure it was not "you" interest did say gays stop protecting him or something like that

Glen Maxey: That guy is a freak. He claims Hillary Clinton murdered people and is a raging lesbian LOL

Glen Maxey: He's a right wing homophobe.

Glen Maxey: Been fighting with me for years on gay rights stuff

Joey the Hustler: No that I believe that but even if she did or is. So what there is not any proof. Heh like anything.

Joey the Hustler: So what did you have in mind?

Glen Maxey: Pay u for a couple of hours to get to know you

Glen Maxey: Take you to dinner if you want

Joey the Hustler: I would like that sometime. But I just can't this week.

Glen Maxey: When you back in Austin? What if I came to Dallas?

Glen Maxey: You still as hot as your pics online?

Joey the Hustler: I really just can't this week.

Joey the Hustler: Always hot..do you look like your pics online?

Glen Maxey: I got pics all over From years ago until now. Old fat guy LOL

Glen Maxey: So when in Austin?

Glen Maxey: I have ideas on how to sell your story, too

Glen Maxey: Small window. Let's talk in person about that

Joey the Hustler: I'm sure you're too hard on yourself.. we should meet like you said. Next week here in Dallas would be ok, I would have to get back with you with time

Glen Maxey: OK

I felt like I'd somehow earned his trust, and even though he did seem to be quite as apolitical as he professed, he seemed to be grasping the importance of his story. And I think he also started to realize that people would pay him a lot of money for that story.

An Initial Perry Attack

The buzzards were starting to circle. Word of my inquiry had gotten around, and now that the Perry campaign had seen an outline of The Journalist's story to refute, I shouldn't have been surprised to see a familiar name pop up in my email.

EMAIL 8/24/2011 8:45 AM From Ken Herman of Austin American-Statesman

Glen,

Perry campaign says these are Facebook messages you posted. Correct?

Thanks.

Ken

> "Glen Maxey July 19 at 9:18pm I'm working on a story with a national reporter on the Rick Perry has homosexual sex story. Just casting a wide net to see what the folks who've been around for decades ever heard. We got some great bullets. Just need to find some more. Glen Maxey"

> And

> "Can you ask around your network of gay men who've been around for a while..... I'm looking for any and all rumors about Rick Perry going back as far as possible. Especially anything prior to the explosion in the media re: Anita filing for divorce for catching him in the act. Key targets are our friends who still

haunt the bars and know a hustler named Joey. Let me know if you ever heard rumors."

As you may recall, Ken Herman was the *Austin American-Statesman* reporter who did the one-on-one interview with Perry to quell the rumors about Perry and Geoff Connor. When this email appeared, my first thought was that this was an obvious repeat of this strategy—the Perry campaign was using Herman to torpedo the story ahead of time. They had sent my two emails that people had forwarded to them to the *Statesman* reporter whose story had helped them the last time.

My supposition was that the Perry campaign was looking for a story about my investigation in an attempt to discredit me before the exposé came out. I figured he would try to lump me in with Robert Morrow and the other people trying to mount an attack. My email conversation with Herman was calculated to try to stop that Perry strategy from working.

EMAIL 8/24/2011 10:35 AM To Ken Herman of **Austin American-Statesman**

Please let me know what story you're working on. A story about Perry? a story about me asking people about Perry? Let's set some on the record and off the record ground rules.

EMAIL 8/24/2011 10:35 From Ken Herman of **Austin American-Statesman**

Sure. At this point I'm not sure what, if anything, I'm writing. Could be a column about people asking about Perry.

EMAIL 8/24/2011 5:31 PM To Ken Herman of **Austin American-Statesman**

Cool. I was worried the Perry Campaign had hijacked you into writing a story about sleazy operatives messing around with their candidate and you comparing me to crazy Robert Morrow and his Chronicle ad.

Before you do their bidding, talk to me.

My message seemed to work. Herman's eventual column focused only on the Morrow ad and not on my investigation.

The Perry campaign set up a meeting in Austin with The Journalist and his publishers to discuss and comment on the story. At the last minute, Perry's people postponed the meeting for a week. This delay was a small relief since The Journalist had a long-scheduled family vacation and I was scheduled to go to New Orleans to volunteer at a health clinic. Moreover, a hurricane was barreling toward the East Coast and New York City. Even a story of a sex scandal wasn't gonna knock Mother Nature off the cable news. The delay was a godsend.

The meeting never happened.

A Lawyer for Joey

Meanwhile, our efforts to get Joey on the record continued.

TEXT 9/1/2011 3:25 PM To Joey the Hustler

Glen Maxey: Hey there. I didn't get to Dallas this week, been playing in New Orleans. I want to take you to dinner and talk. Will pay for your time. Or u in Austin next week? Can you call me? Glen Maxey

Glen Maxey: National press are going to write story about perry. If u get named u need to be ready to deal. Let me help u on this. I have much experience from my past as lobbyist and legislator. Call me.

Joey the Hustler: I'm with client all day.

Glen Maxey: Call at convenience. Even late night.

Glen Maxey: I can even get u a lawyer for free to advise. I want to help.

I talked to lawyer friends to try to find someone who would represent Joey, and help protect his interests, legal and financial. I also was pretty sure that one of the national publications or players nosing around the Perry story might be willing to pay Joey for an exclusive exposé — particularly after the Larry Flynt million dollar offer surfaced.

Meanwhile, by now Perry had skyrocketed ahead of Romney and the rest of the field in the polls. Joey seemed to be aware that his story value might have risen dramatically.

Glen Maxey: I will also continue discussions with folks who would buy story.

Glen Maxey: The money is in the story details.

Glen Maxey: I want to talk ten minutes by phone asap when you can. To lay out the plan to get folks into bidding war for your details.

Joey the Hustler: from my understanding that something that an attorney would handle. if im to speak of this it would have to be within guaranteed confidence at least in the beginning. I'm not an attorney I do not fully understand what my exposure is.

Glen Maxey: That is why I want you to have the best attorney. And also that would give you ability to refer anyone trying to contact you to do so through your attorney. Gives you protection. And let's you negotiate deals.

Glen Maxey: Call me.

Soon an excellent attorney, "Joey's Austin Lawyer," surfaced who agreed to talk to Joey. Joey's legal protection seemed to be coming together.

Of course I couldn't control what Joey and his lawyer decided to do. In theory, I thought, they could have sold Joey's silence to Perry. Nevertheless, I thought that Joey was surprisingly unsophisticated in such matters and he should be protected, whatever the result.

All the while, Perry continued throwing rhetorical red meat to the Republican base. He even told social conservatives that nothing in his personal life would "embarrass" them. That struck me as strange. It sounded almost like Gary Hart's infamous dare in the face of rumors he might have had an extramarital affair: "Follow me around. I don't care. … If anybody wants to put a tail on me, go ahead." They did—and he got caught and self-destructed. Was Perry trying to do the same thing? He certainly motivated me.

TEXT 9/2/2011 5:42 PM To Joey the Hustler

Glen Maxey: At you earliest opportunity call [Joey's Austin Lawyer]. He is your attorney. He will talk to you about [National Attorney] . She wants to represent you. She will make you a LOT of money. [National Attorney] is a lawyer who is always on TV with high profile clients

Glen Maxey: The attorneys will protect you.

Glen Maxey: I won't bother you anymore once I know you have a private attorney.

Glen Maxey: Please confirm that you have called [Joey's Austin Lawyer] so I will quit worrying about you.

No response. I was worried about what was happening to Joey.

In fact, Joey's attorney had indeed enlisted National Attorney to shore up the case and show the nation that Joey meant business. She was enthused, and wanted to take the case.

However, it turned out that by this point Joey still hadn't called either attorney.

The Journalist and his editors had mixed feelings about National Attorney's involvement. The Journalist worried that she might make the entire story be taken less seriously, and as just another one of her headline-grabbing ploys. His editor, however, described it as "fucking awesome."

Her stature did help legitimize the case, legitimize Joey, and seemed to increase the odds that the story would run before the Iowa caucuses.

With the wildly fluctuating poll results, Joey's team seemed to have a strong incentive to finalize their financial or other arrangements for him as soon as possible. If Perry dropped in the polls, presumably his story value would, too.

The days of communication blackout from Joey caused me to worry. Had the Perry camp bought his silence? Had he decided that he was not up for any national publicity? Had his cell phone just died?

Regardless of his responsiveness or willingness to play ball, The Journalist told me that Joey was still in the story, even without his on-the-record statement. The Journalist said he had several other people on the record corroborating stories about Joey, James, and Geoff Connor. He also had Joey on the record from their first brief phone conversation together saying things like "I could retire if I sold this story."

9/5/2011 EMAIL 8:30 PM From The Journalist

Let's regroup early tomorrow and figure out what to do about [Joey.]

9/5/2011 EMAIL 8:33PM To The Journalist

cool. I'm going to text him again tonight re: contacting the attorney

9/5/2011 EMAIL 8:42 PM From The Journalist

K.

9/5/2011 EMAIL 8:42 PM From The Journalist

All you need from [Joey] is a time and place to meet. Either in Austin or Dallas?

9/5/2011 EMAIL 8:45 PM To The Journalist

And you have an idea of making that happen without a lawyer offer or money offer?
Ain't. gonna. happen.
I know it.

9/5/2011 EMAIL 8:47 PM To The Journalist

He needs a deadline. And we ain't got one.

If I could tell him the story is gonna run on X date and he has only X days to get his ducks in a row with lawyers, et al.
Then he might move on the plan.

9/5/2011 EMAIL 8:55PM From The Journalist

7 days. 7 days to get ducks in a row. story is running in two weeks tops. I can get a firmer date.

9/5/2011 EMAIL 8:55 PM To The Journalist

I'll tell him that.... generally. Less than 7 days to get his ducks in a row or have his goose cooked.

The Journalist—and his publishers—were ready to fly down to any place in Texas at any time to get his story on the record.

We crossed our fingers that Joey would resume contact.

TEXTS 9/6/20111:40 AM To Joey the Hustler

Glen Maxey: Hope you had a good weekend.

Glen Maxey: The perry story is going to run early next week. You and I are both in it and we will be besieged by press.

Glen Maxey: If you are not back in Austin till weekend we could set something up for Sunday. But that's probably as last as you'd want to wait.

No response. The Journalist and I had to start thinking about backup plans.

EMAIL 9/6/2011 2:28 PM From The Journalist

Glen:

Worst cases I've been thinking about: 1) We get the lawyer to put in a call directly to [Joey] at the end of the week; 2) I fly down on Sunday and we just start looking for him--i.e. go to his house.

What do you think?

EMAIL 9/6/2011 2:31 PM To The Journalist

Sure. Don't know the ethics of lawyers "ambulance chasing" here. Guess it's not really soliciting a case after an accident, since nothing here was done on accident.

I'm tied up all day Saturday with gay pride events (morning through 6 pm). Otherwise, I am free.

It would be good to know that he's actually come back to Austin.

EMAIL 9/6/2011 2:28 PM From The Journalist

OK. Maybe we hold off on the lawyer call. Hoping we hear from [Joey] in the next FOUR days.

Robby Appears, Disappears

Out of the blue, Robby, the Governor's office staffer who supposedly was fired in an anti-gay purge of the office following the Connor affair, called The Journalist back, after a month of silence. We'd never been able to find his name on the rolls of anyone who worked for the Governor's office. The Journalist still wanted to prove that Robby had worked there in some capacity and had understood that he was fired because, as we had heard that he put it, "Perry got a blow job."

EMAIL 9/6/2011 8:23 PM From The Journalist

Subject: [Robby]

He called me tonight to tell me to leave him alone. I did get to ask him about how his name wasn't on any employee rolls. He said: "I know." I asked why. He said: "That's none of your business." He said he wanted to leave Austin behind him.

EMAIL 9/6/2011 8:27 PM To The Journalist

Very weird.

I keep getting a suspicion that he was interning the Governor. If you get my drift. And that's why there's the confidentiality agreement.

EMAIL 9/6/2011 8:28 PM From The Journalist

I agree. The other thing that's weird: if he wanted me to stop calling him, why could he just say: You got it all wrong. I never worked for Perry.

Robby's non-denial response never made sense. Why would an intern, or some other low-level lackey, have to sign a confidentiality agreement that prohibited him from even saying that he worked in the Governor's office? Something about Robby's responses didn't add up.

If it wasn't true, if he wasn't fired for being gay or from some concern that he might be, if he didn't know anything, why not just deny it all or explain what happened?

Joey Responds

Joey finally responded.

TEXTS 9/7/2011 1:00 PM From Joey the Hustler

Joey the Hustler: Just got back to my phone. why all of sudden the urgency? What is going on with these other guys?

Glen Maxey: The urgency is just that the story runs in less than a week. And I just thought you should get lawyer lined up before

Cause when it mentions he might have been a client, Then you are going to get money offers. And u need attorney to shop u the biggest deal.

Twenty minutes passed, and Joey didn't respond. I wasn't sure what he meant by "other guys." Other Perry hookups we had heard about? Other reporters? Lawyers?

That night was the first Republican debate featuring Rick Perry. He had famously dodged all debates with his Democratic gubernatorial opponent Bill White in the 2010 cycle. I attended a large gathering of Austin liberals to watch the event and boo Perry's performance.

He was a terrible debater, just awesomely awful, when faced with actual opponents challenging his views and moderators unwilling to lob nice, slow softballs at him. I understood why he'd fought so hard to avoid debating White last cycle.

At the time, Perry was riding high atop the national polls, with some surveys showing a double-digit lead over Romney. He was cracking 30% in a crowded race. I was convinced that he would be the nominee. Little did I know how convincingly he soon would imitate a dropping rock in the polls.

Focus On Joey

The Journalists and his editor seemed increasingly obsessed on Joey. He was their key puzzle part. His affidavit their silver bullet.

I told The Journalist that protecting his ass was all fine and good, but sitting on the story and not forcing Perry to acknowledge or refute it wasn't acceptable. If they weren't ballsy enough to run with it, then it was time for me to take the story elsewhere.

By now I had heard from *National Enquirer*, and I believed that they were ready to pay Joey for his story. I emailed and texted him to try to get him to call his lawyer to pursue that relationship. I felt that if I could ever talk to him in person, I could seal the deal and make everyone happy.

I learned that Joey was coming back to town on the weekend, I knew where he lived, and I was willing to go over there if I had to.

I tried again to reach Joey—and I had more success than ever before.

TEXT 9/8/2011 3:04 AM To Joey the Hustler

Glen Maxey: [National Enquirer says] they will pay handsomely to anyone who can tell them they have been with Rick Perry.

Glen Maxey: Call your attorney and I will connect him to these guys at Enquirer.

Glen Maxey: If I were u I would take it and head to the Islands.

I wasn't sure what else I could say to just get him to call his lawyer. He needed protection, and not of the latex kind.

Joey the Hustler: How much traction do you think this is going to get really... life is a valuable thing don't you think that is at risk here? It's not about money. Where are you getting these numbers? Nothing worthwhile is ever cheap.

Did he still really not understand or care about the potential national importance of this story?

Glen Maxey: I think staying out of sight is a bigger risk.

Glen Maxey: Having legal protection is good no matter if you sell story or not

Glen Maxey: We are in the [National News Outlet] story no matter what we do

Glen Maxey: You want to go to meet lawyer together?

Glen Maxey: Or you and I just meet privately to talk this through?

Glen Maxey: I am available to help

I didn't want to scare him, but we needed to hurry this up.

Joey the Hustler: I don't have any time to go back to aus that I can see in this time frame. This will have little traction in the press I feel. Don't you remember the last report about him an an escort aired one night and was killed.

Joey the Hustler: If it does it could get interesting.

Glen Maxey: That was about hookup with the gay secretary of state

It was interesting to me to hear how he thought that the Connor story was "killed." While arguably the *Austin American Statesman* had given Perry an effective platform to deny it, the story was still very much alive in Austin's GLBT and political circles. And I couldn't fault the press back then completely—I and The Journalist personally had learned just how difficult and maddeningly frustrating it could be to try to get everything put together and stay together.

Joey the Hustler: I am going to have to take time for a phone meeting with these attorneys to at least say "hello"

Glen Maxey: He is front runner for President. Lots more eyes on him

Glen Maxey: Call them. Get protected legally as least

Glen Maxey: Then work through the rest

Joey the Hustler: I am more then likely the least political person you will ever meet... I didn't even know he was running for head figure head.

He didn't know Perry was running for "head figure head"? Astounding. For someone with so much "life" experience, Joey was politically clueless and way off the grid. But, then again, maybe he was pretty sharp, or justifiably cynical, if he thought the President of the United States today is just a figurehead.

Glen Maxey: And if necessary [your lawyers] would meet u in Dallas. It is that big.

Joey the Hustler: I have very little to say unless I am fully protected.

Glen Maxey: Then get the fucking attorney locked down.

Glen Maxey: Will You please?

Joey the Hustler: Why do you care? What will you get out of this?

Glen Maxey: I get a clean conscience that you don't get fucked over. I am political. I did talk to reporters and guys who found u.

Glen Maxey: So just want to take care and be concerned about your well being.

I could have just sold his story and all of the sources to the *National Enquirer* or a web-based tabloid. I didn't. We were holding up the story in part to get Joey on the record and in part to get him the legal protection that would enable his story to come out on the record.

Joey the Hustler: That's not all tell me more

Glen Maxey: About what? Me?

Joey the Hustler: It's no matter.. how did you hear this?

Glen Maxey: I hate Perry's hypocrisy. I have been a gay rights leader for thirty years. Perry will be really bad for us. People with AIDS.

Glen Maxey: You told story years ago to some guys in Rain. They told another guy. Then that guy told a friend of mine.

Joey the Hustler: Well no comment. But it is what it is…Have you and I met in person?

Glen Maxey: Never

Glen Maxey: Only know u through these texts and your postings on web

Joey the Hustler: I just changed them LOL. I am sure this will have an interesting affect on my side biz

Glen Maxey: LOL, like I said, u could retire to the islands.

Joey the Hustler: Looks like I might have to

Glen Maxey: Not the worst thing to happen LOL

Joey the Hustler: The press is not a bed of roses I am sure

Glen Maxey: But you can control the story on your terms or let them pick u apart. I am going to control what happens to me.

Joey the Hustler: they're going to have a field day regardless. I will contact [Joey's Austin Lawyer] before sat.

Glen Maxey: Good I will sleep well tonight

Joey the Hustler: Speaking of. I have to be up in about 4 hours.

Glen Maxey: Me too Take care. Keep me posted. And I will let you know what I hear. Do you check email? Or texts better?

Our conversation ended there, at 4:30 a.m. on September 8.

Later that morning, I relayed the conversation to The Journalist and passed it on to Joey's attorney.

It was our most promising conversation yet. Joey came across as credible and honest. The Journalist agreed with my impression that Joey was scared, but felt that he trusted me now. He was testing me a bit, but he seemed to believe me. Hard to fault a career hustler for not believing every man who comes along with publication proposals about presidential candidates, possible book deals, and legal protection. His consent to finally call the lawyer was a signal to me that he'd eventually give his statement on the record.

EMAIL 9/8/2011 6:26 PM The Journalist

Any word from the National Enquirer?

EMAIL 9/8/2011 6:26 PM To The Journalist

Any word on [National News Outlet?]

My attorney and I shall be listening to the National Enquirer in a Sunday phone call. Emphasis on listenting.

I'm still not buying the line that if you get a statement from Joey, that the story sits for two weeks.

No way.

EMAIL 9/8/2011 6:27 PM From The Journalist

We get a statement from Joey, we're running the story in days not weeks. You are right.

EMAIL 9/8/2011 6:29 PM To The Journalist

He said before Saturday. It's not Saturday.

EMAIL 9/8/2011 6:46 PM From The Journalist

Point is I realize that I have to be patient and just wait. I feel like [Joey] has something to say. Just need to wait till lawyer call. How do you feel about [Joey,] waiting, etc.

EMAIL 9/8/2011 7:15 PM To The Journalist

Just one question for you. Who the hell held your hand when your baby was about to be born? God, they must have taken a bottle of tranquilizers just to listen to you yammer and worry. LOL

Patience, grasshopper.

EMAIL 9/8/2011 7:26 PM From The Journalist

Look: half my day is spent thinking about this story. I woke up this morning--in fact every morning--hoping you have sent me a late-night email disclosing a [Joey] text.

Pathetic?

Just want this story done and published as bad as you do.

National Enquirer

On Saturday, my attorney and I had a phone call with a leading *National Enquirer* reporter. I knew they were interested in the story. I assumed that Joey's story would be a natural for them. Despite the tortured path that The Journalist's publication had taken me down, I still hoped that it would break the story. *National Enquirer* seemed more likely to want a feature story on an alleged Perry partner, like Joey, rather than an in-depth, wide-ranging investigation such as The Journalist was pursuing so doggedly.

My expectation proved right. *National Enquirer* had established considerable street cred with its path-breaking/campaign-breaking work on the John Edwards story. It was clear they knew their business and had well-developed, careful investigative and financial procedures. That included a proposed contract, and a full-court super-fast investigative effort. They could be on the scene immediately. They clearly wanted a story like Joey's.

I was somewhat conflicted. By now, I liked The Journalist. We had worked so long and so hard together. I was convinced that he wanted the truth and only the truth, but that his motives were good and he was incredibly persevering in the face of seemingly innumerable obstacles we had worked to overcome. He was a serious journalist, and I hoped he'd get the story.

On the other hand, as I tried to imagine Joey's perspective and interests, one thing was obvious—The Journalist could not and would not pay anything for the story. That's not the way his publication operated. Joey might need protection. He might need to leave Texas. He might need to pay lawyers. *National Enquirer* or some other national media outlet that could provide some sort of reasonable compensation was probably much more important to him and perhaps to his lawyers.

I hoped that both options could work. Maybe a *National Enquirer* cover story one day, and then an in-depth story by The Journalist the next. To me, that was an ideal solution. However, as I well knew, the ideal rarely becomes the real.

9/11/2011 TEXTS *Glen Maxey and Joey the Hustler*

Glen Maxey: Everything go ok with your lawyer? You get linked up? Just checking in since I did not hear back from you.

Joey the Hustler: We talked. I am still looking at options. It's a weekend so I am going place to place. I appreciate your concern and assistance.

I was relieved to hear that they'd connected. Joey had representation now, and I hoped that he and his lawyers would handle things now. Maybe I could relax.

Glen Maxey: Cool. You coming back to Austin? We should have dinner just to get beyond our "text" level friendship.

Joey the Hustler: I would like that sometime. I am supposed to go to Florida but I may cancel. We will see.

Glen Maxey: Great. I wouldn't take off till you decide about selling your story. Lots of money about to be offered to you, I know. But talk to your lawyer, not [my] business.

Joey the Hustler: Would it not be better for me to have an attorney that is a perry supporter?

Glen Maxey: No way. They will screw you over to protect him.

Joey the Hustler: Nothing is free. What is there real motive or personal agenda…

Glen Maxey: Do not understand last sentence? Motive or agenda?

Glen Maxey: The people paying want to sell newspapers, etc.

Joey the Hustler: I see that... I am talking about [my lawyers]. Nothing is ever free they have a motive and agenda just as we all do.

Joey the Hustler: Ok good luck.

Talking to Joey's Austin Lawyer

More time passed. I decided to call Joey's Austin Lawyer to explain the background of the story and underscore what I perceived to be the urgency. We should not underestimate Perry's potential ineptitude on the campaign trail—if only I had known how true that was!—and I thought that Joey and his lawyers needed to move quickly.

I hoped my message got through. Disturbingly, though, I got the sense from his lawyer that Joey wasn't sure if he wanted to talk yet. Joey's clock moved at a different speed from mine.

Competition on the Trail

Two days later, I got a lengthy email that gave me and The Journalist great worry. Another Texas Newspaper Reporter whom I knew from my time at the Capitol was closing in on our story. This was the first time I'd heard heavy footsteps around some of our more underground sources.

EMAIL 9/13/2011 11:42 PM From Texas Newspaper Reporter

I have spoken to about 4 people who have guy friends who they say have had romantic flings with Rick Perry. The problem is that their friends are terrified of speaking/telling about it. At least one of them has gone into hiding .....after speaking to [National News Outlet] on grounds of confidentiality.

One of my 30-year-long friends works next to Charlies. She is close to one of the long-time bartenders there. He apparently knows something about RP. She has tried to arrange a meeting with her friend, herself and me. So far, no go.

Another person, active in Austin's gay community, tells me that his friend's ex had a thing going with Perry when he was ag commissioner. But, so far, neither he nor his friend's ex has been able to convince the corporate executive to talk to me.

He also mentioned Former Legislator, and other sources who had given their friends' stories to us on the record. The Journalist and I talked about what we could legitimately do to slow down this new competition. Eventually I sent him the names of every source we knew of who apparently had intel but wouldn't give it up to us—Anita Perry's former co-workers during the Geoff Connor incident, elected officials who seemed to know something but were reticent to spill, and a variety of other leads that we had not been able to crack. Heck, maybe he'd succeed where we failed, but if not, that might keep him busy for long enough to let our story break.

And remember that guy Bob, whose friend called Perry his "Sugar Daddy"? When I followed up with Texas Newspaper Reporter, he told me that another reporter, a colleague of his, had met the same source a few years earlier at a party, where the source had claimed he'd had a sexual encounter with Perry. Unfortunately, this second reporter was shortly thereafter shipped out to an embed in the Middle East and hadn't followed up. Texas Newspaper Reporter asked his colleague to reach out to the host of the party and get contact information for the party guest. The host said the source wasn't around anymore and that he'd gone AWOL after The Journalist and I talked to him.

Two independently working journalists had found the same source, and now that source had gone off the grid.

More Non-Progress

Once again, The Journalist asked me to follow up with Joey. I was to do whatever I could to coax Joey into telling his story. I should convince him that he could trust his lawyer and The Journalist because I trusted them, and that it was now or never.

TEXT MESSAGES 9/13/2011 6:10 PM With Joey the Hustler

Glen Maxey: [National News Outlet] is holding the story for a week so you have your lawyer stuff all lined up. Hope that helps u. Is that working out OK? You met them? Keep me posted.

Joey the Hustler: What do they say or are saying so far? I am sure you know some you can share

Glen Maxey: [Your] attorneys? They can't talk to me. Lawyer / Client privilege. What you and they talk about or what is happening with them could only be disclosed by u

Glen Maxey: Or with your approval.

Glen Maxey: Have you met in person?

Joey the Hustler: Not yet.

Glen Maxey: Hope that happens soon. Ask them to do so. I am sure they are waiting on u.

Joey the Hustler: It's all good.

Glen Maxey: ok That is what I wanted to hear.

Joey the Hustler: So what did your sources say about my story?

Glen Maxey: All I know is fourth hand. That you were hired three or four times a year by aide to governor to play with them at local hotel. T hat is about it.

Joey the Hustler: no comment on specifics. I've been told not to talk with anybody..

Glen Maxey: Gotcha. Sorry. I should not have asked.

Joey the Hustler: But I do hope they don't print anything specific because more than likely it would be in the wrong.

Glen Maxey: They cannot unless you tell them.

Glen Maxey: Talk to your attorney about what to tell [The Journalist.]

Glen Maxey: So he doesn't say anything wrong. That is how I would control that.

Glen Maxey: In other words, I would give [National News Outlet] a statement of confirmation. Let them run it with the other guy's stories

Joey the Hustler: I don't really feel any pressure here.

Glen Maxey: If [National News Outlet] writes incorrect stuff it could mushroom though.

Glen Maxey: I don't now what u and [The Journalist] talked about weeks ago. So u have a better handle on what he might write.

Joey the Hustler: If there is anything incorrect it will mushroom badly.

Glen Maxey: I agree. Talk to your lawyers about getting you with [The Journalist] to get that locked down. I know [The Journalist] would fly to wherever u want to do so.

Glen Maxey: Last thing they want in a story this big is inaccurate stuff.

Joey felt "no pressure." I could not understand his sense of timing. Worse, I wasn't sure that he did.

I also knew that Joey's Austin Lawyer couldn't tell me anything without Joey's permission. I at least was glad to see that Joey had also been given the advice, and heeded it, not to spill the details of what was going on with his lawyer to me.

On the plus side, Joey was clearly concerned about what the various publications were going to write and if it was going to be accurate or not. He was clearly good at negotiating and getting information out of me. Maybe he was using that skill behind the scene with other media and I just didn't know.

TEXT MESSAGES 9/13/2011 7:30 PM With Joey the Hustler

Joey the Hustler: Thanks for your help. S tay in touch. We should meet one day.

Glen Maxey: If you need me for moral support or whatever in meetings just say the word. I am retired and can be there at drop of hat.

Glen Maxey: Call me when in Austin. I will buy you dinner.

Joey the Hustler: your sweet thank you..

Nice—but more non-progress.

The Competition, Again

The other reporter who'd honed in on our sources was also following some of the same trails as I was, which had arguably been smoothed out by some of my investigative work. I hadn't told him anything we'd found, but it was useful to see that he was coming up with the same stories through his network.

FACEBOOK MESSAGE 9/15/2011 From Texas Newspaper Reporter

My SA friend has a friend close to the DPS trooper allegedly in the mansion when Anita allegedly found Perry with Conner. He (allegedly) witnessed the blowup....and Conner coming down from upstairs. But he apparently has only told close friends - and is not approachable because he fears for his pension, his job and having someone plant drugs on him.

Our other guy has gone underground since talking to you guys. He's gone - for us.

We are not making much progress. Another guy has not been able to get his friend's friend to talk to us.

Geoff Conner has not replied to my msg that I sent to his Facebook page.

It's getting frustrating. This could take many months. I don't have many months.

Many months? I'd started this process on June 23rd, and it was now mid September.

Restless Natives

Political insiders were growing impatient. An anonymous person found
The Journalist's email address and sent him the following missive:

Date: Thu, Sep 15, 2011 at 4:39 PM
Subject: what's taking so long (Gay Rick Perry)
To: The Journalist

Dear [The Journalist],

It's already all over Texas that you and Glen Maxey spent a week in
Austin rooting out gay men who'd go on (or off) the record about having
sex with Rick Perry. What's the hold up on publishing the story?

Three men have been polygraphed and passed, they have retained a
lawyer, so what's the [National News Outlet] lawyer waiting for, Perry to
admit it?

~A fan in Texas

I joked that one of my impatient friends must have sent it.

Meanwhile, the rumor mill was getting out of control. I'd heard that an
attorney friend had done a polygraph of three men who'd had encounters
with Perry (not true). A friend's friend got a call from a Texas newspaper
asking if she'd helped set up dalliances for Perry in New York City.

Here in Texas, everyone was trying to hop on the Perry gravy train. His
candidacy was great for Texas newspapers. A slew of reporters and
consultants were trying to sell books on the real Rick Perry.

I heard that Former Legislator himself–the man outed in his criminal trial, who we thought had something about his dalliances with Perry in his divorce case, but to no avail thus far– was thinking about selling his memoirs.

Meanwhile, Romney was starting to inch back in the polls, as Perry started dropping. Perry no longer seemed a slam-dunk. On the upside, a drawn-out nomination might buy us more time to get Joey on the record. On the downside, if Perry continued falling in the polls, our story might disappear.

The Journalist and Joey's Lawyers

Then progress seemed likely in The Journalist's dealings with Joey's lawyers. The Journalist was ready to hop the next flight to Texas to meet with Joey in person, verify his story, and hit "publish" on the exposé. We were so close—once again.

Joey's Lawyer told The Journalist that Joey was a "very credible" guy and that Joey wanted to go forward and receive reasonable compensation. However, he also said that Joey was scared for his safety. Joey thought that The Journalist's story was the strongest and wanted that to be published first, since the added information The Journalist had on James and Geoff Connor would enhance his own credibility.

I was so relieved to hear this progress. Joey was listening. He understood that his position was stronger if The Journalists broke the story first. My ideal scenario would be real.

But then another day passed. The Journalist still hadn't landed Joey. We were stalled again.

EMAIL 9/23/2011 9:33 AM From The Journalist

Subject: ugh! One more email from me!

Glen:

-----Sorry to spam you this morning. One other thought: Can you renew your texting w/ [Joey] and see if you can get him talking about Perry? Like did you know who he was when you all hooked up?

-----I'm thinking that we have two other options if the lawyer shuts us out. One: we run those texts. The other option: We try to get [Joey] to confirm what's already in our story and sign affidavit. He's not technically talking to us. He already talked to us. Someone else can get "exclusive interview."

-----We, after all, already talked to him.

Just thinking out loud here.

Still want meeting with [Joey.]

Fox Gnaws on Perry

I'd spent the day watching Fox News. The hosts were shredding Perry. My years working on campaigns told me that when the corporate masters of the Republican Party turned on you, your days were numbered. A poll from Rasmussen, a Republican-leaning polling firm, had Perry's lead down to just 4 points over Romney. His plummet velocity was approaching warp speed.

On the plus side, that meant that a well-timed story within the week might grab headlines and perhaps even finish his candidacy.

On the down side, we might have very little time for our story to make a meaningful contribution to the national discourse on Perry's candidacy.

The Drop-Dead Tactic

The Journalist told me he was ready to run the story, even without anything else from Joey. He'd suggested to his editors that they fact-check everything around Joey's story and go with that. If the drop-dead timeline sped things up with Joey's lawyers, so be it.

We decided to take this last weekend to let Joey's lawyers sort it out. If that didn't work, on Monday the story would go forward.

That night, Herman Cain won the Florida straw poll.

TEXT MESSAGES 9/25/2011 5:12 PM With Joey The Hustler

Glen Maxey: Hey guy, everything going ok?

Glen Maxey: Perry was flying high in polls. Now he messed up. I wouldn't wait if u want to sell a story. He may be out of the race.

Glen Maxey: Bet u never would have dreamed all this was possible outcome when u hooked up with him back then.

Joey the Hustler: The whole thing is crazy.

Glen Maxey: Crazy yes. U should take advantage of it.

My mentor and former boss in the Texas Senate, Oscar Mauzy, always said about bad legislation, "When you see a snake in the grass, and you have the hoe in your hand, you chop the mother fucking snake's head off. Don't wait." The snake's campaign was wounded already. Running the story might chop its head off once and for all.

The Journalist could print the story within twenty-four hours, with the three strongest incidents and some twenty people talking on the record about various incidents and rumors. It was the best story with which to do the deed. But at this point, I almost didn't care. I just wanted the hoe to chop—something, finally. I was exhausted.

I sent a final entreaty to Joey's lawyers: "Talk me off this ledge. Tell me your client and National News Outlet and Flynt or National Enquirer [that you] are going to do something. Before I do something rash."

Preparing for the worst, I'd begun working privately to set up a website where I could publish my investigation and ask readers to submit other relevant information. I'd read plenty of comments on blogs from people who'd professed detailed knowledge of Perry's encounters. Some of those tales matched pretty closely other Perry stories I'd heard. That was another possibility: Publishing anything might open the floodgates for other truth-tellers.

Yet another day passed with no news. I was beginning to think that involving the attorneys was a bad strategic decision on my part. I might have been able to get The Journalist to run the story by now without them.

My own lawyer thought I'd done the right thing, at least. Trying to help Joey protect himself and receive fair compensation still seemed the right thing to have done, even if his lawyers perhaps delayed the story. I had no reason to doubt their sincerity or competence, but all I could see is that they hadn't gotten Joey to the finish line.

The Journalist was trying to get Joey to give his full name to them on the record. Meanwhile, I'd already given The Journalist's publication his name and his dick size. Really, what more do you need? What's with modern journalistic standards? But I had also supplied Joey's phone number,

123

email, and residence address—and photos, in all types of poses and arousals. Talk about extended research. The Journalist had it all.

At that point, I wasn't sure why getting Joey on the record became the Holy Grail for National News Outlet. I was convinced that they were willing to do the story without him on the record until Perry's lawyers threatened them. But the idea of Perry suing a major multinational media firm like The Journalist's seemed far-fetched. Can you imagine the depositions the media lawyers (or mine) could have taken from Perry, Connor, Joey, James, Charlie's Bar bartenders, and on and on? How much would those transcripts sell for?

Stalled

Another day, and then another week. Herman Cain surged in the polls. Joey's Austin Lawyer indicated through the grapevine that I needed to cool my jets.

The Journalist wanted the story to run as much as I did. The first week in October was—once again—to be the last week he would wait. How many times had I heard that by now? Wednesday, he'd call Joey's lawyers and demand they fact-check the story. The new goal was to finish everything by Friday.

After he started talking to his lawyers, Joey became less responsive to me. My complaining may have spooked them. I'd ask him how he was doing, and he'd respond "I'm not at liberty to say." I'd offer to get together and buy him dinner at the fancy place he liked downtown and he'd demur. I felt like the lawyers had seized control of his life. To what end? I wasn't sure.

EMAIL 10/10/2011 4:29 PM From The Journalist

Writing story. It's due on Wednesday. Gonna try our best to run this.

EMAIL 10/10/2011 5:06 PM To The Journalist

Due on Wednesday means what? Another three weeks with [the publishers]?

EMAIL 10/10/2011 5:07 PM From The Journalist

I turn in a draft on Wednesday. Then we bring it to [the publisher].

The Journalist decided that in lieu of Joey, they'd use me as a literary device to get to Joey and use our communications to show his story.

I felt some irony in that just two months earlier, when Perry was preparing to announce and the rumors were swirling anew, I was beating off reporters with a stick. Everyone wanted to know what I knew. But I stuck with The Journalist. I patiently (at first) and then impatiently but loyally kept waiting for his story to run. I was convinced that he was a true investigative journalist, well-motivated, and would not be deterred from achieving the goal—an accurate story, compellingly told, and, I hoped, devastatingly truthful and effective.

Then a friend put me in touch with a *New York Times* reporter who had a history of breaking sex scandals in the national paper of record. I talked to him. I told him the stories, and explained where we were with The Journalist's publications. I told him that if the story didn't run, I would turn all of my notes over to him next week.

I told The Journalist about my conversation with the *Times.* That seemed to light a fire under him. He reworked the story extensively. He said he would base the Joey section on my and Joey's text message exchanges, as well as the third-party verification from folks to whom Joey had told his story. After all his effort, The Journalist clearly did not want to get scooped.

Success!!!

On October 12, The Journalist turned the story in.

His editor signed off on the final story.

The chief news editor signed off.

We were almost at the money shot.

The very last step was for the publisher of National News Outlet to approve. How could she possibly fail to do so when their top reporter and all editors had approved?

Naturally, she was out of the country.

I was orally read The Journalist's story over the phone. It was magnificent. The lede started:

> *"Presidential candidate Rick Perry of Texas has had sex with at least two men during his time as Governor, an investigation by National News Outlet has confirmed."*

The story detailed the experiences of Joey, James, and the Geoff Connor story, with new on-the-record sources detailing what those three individuals' friends and networks said about the incidents. It didn't have Joey the Hustler's slam-dunk affidavit, but the story was solid and exhaustively researched. I felt that any objective reader would be convinced that Rick Perry had had homosexual sex with men. I could not imagine any way that Perry's forces could discredit all of the sources that The Journalist cited and relied on.

Success was inevitable.

But … No, it wasn't.

Failure

The publisher of National News Outlet again refused to run the story. Without Joey on the record, she balked. All of the other sources, all of the corroboration, all of the exhaustive research—all of that failed to satisfy her, despite the unanimous approval of her writing and editorial staff.

Why?

I heard different stories about why the publisher blinked and failed to back up her staff and editors and surrendered to Perry's threats. I guess no one knows for sure why she did that. What follows is but my own idle speculation.

National News Outlet used to be an independent company. Now it's owned by a mega-corporation. "Courageous in-house counsel" is a phrase so oxymoronic that it's hard to say without laughing. Did mega-corp's lawyers wimp out and pull rank on the publisher? That wouldn't be surprising. Corporate uberlords rarely criticize their in-house legal team for failing to lead the company into risky territory. What's the upside for the lawyers in doing that?

The publisher is famously tough. Perry's camp had threatened to sue National News Outlet earlier along the way in this story's tortuous path— and that only seemed to increase her resolve to run with the story if it panned out.

My speculation ranged to more sinister explanations. Mega-corporations of a feather tend to flock together. Perry, while riding high in the polls, had a flock of major business owners supporting him.

But who knows? I'm sure I'll never know the specific reason for the corporate/journalistic decision not to run the Perry story.

Aftermath

With independent publication by National News Outlet off the table again, I briefly shopped the story to other outlets. But when they too all started chirping about an affidavit from Joey, I realized that I had no desire or remaining energy to pursue that perhaps unattainable Holy Grail. If the professional writing and editorial staff of National News Outlet had concluded that the Grail was unnecessary, why should I continue that effort?

Then, on October 18, Perry floundered in yet another debate. His campaign became like a guided missile targeted to crash to earth as quickly as possible. The value of Joey's story dropped accordingly. The Holy Grail seemed to be sinking over the horizon.

I and The Journalist both shopped some other potential story publishers, but Perry's self-inflicted impending demise seemed to be his best defense against this story.

Then on October 30, I saw that Politico.com broke the story about Herman Cain harassing a woman while he worked for the National Restaurant Association. Politico ran the entire story—and based it almost entirely on anonymous sources. Where were the on-the-record quotes I was required to have? Why didn't they need to have two dozen people speaking openly about what they'd heard or known?

As time passed, I pondered the standards that journalism applies to gay-story sources, to gay hustlers. My analysis left me troubled. But it also left me determined to write down this chronicle of my experiences. Perhaps this will be useful to others in the future. Perhaps it won't.

Part IV: What It Takes

What does it take to "out" a powerful, career politician, even if he is one of the biggest homophobic hypocrites in history? What if he has had homosexual relationships but decides to run for president on an increasingly anti-gay platform that would reinstate overt discrimination in the military and in society at large?

How many sources have to tell their stories and how many have to do so on the record for the story to be published?

And if the best source is a gay hustler, an almost painfully naïve young man who didn't even know Rick Perry was running for President, will anyone ever believe him, even if he told his story to friends at a time when Rick Perry was an inconsequential minor political figure?

More broadly, what are the standards and burdens of proof that modern media apply in deciding when to publish, and when not to publish, such a story? And what potential consequences for the nation turn on the press's decision on whether or not to publish?

The almost-six-month investigation that consumed my entire life was sparked by a simple curiosity: Could I discover and prove the truth concerning the many, many stories and rumors that Rick Perry had sex with men?

After the immediate success of finding two men with separate knowledge of a hustler who said that he hooked up with Perry, what kept my inquiry going—and what in turn drove so many people to share what they knew—was Perry's astonishing and increasing hostility toward GLBT issues.

I said at the beginning of this book that I set out to answer two questions through my investigation: Has Rick Perry had sex with men? And if so, can I prove it?

Has Rick Perry had sex with men? Personally, I believe he has. The strength and volume of stories and witnesses are to me very, very convincing. To recap, here are the alleged same-sex encounters described in this book:

- Four random men at gay bars who told me personally that they or their friend had hooked up with Perry
- A young male hustler who told friends and me that he had sex on multiple occasions with Perry and his friends
- A man who claimed to have answered a Craigslist Ad and ended up having sex with Perry
- A man with his pinkie finger in Perry's belt loop at a gay party
- A Former Legislator who had encounters with Perry at a legislative conference
- A guy who called Perry his "Sugar Daddy" and disappeared when a reporter merely questioned him about it
- A widely rumored relationship with an official appointed to statewide office, which exploded into the public
- A curious set of three young gay men who allegedly were "rearranged" from jobs at the Capitol ostensibly for being gay— one of whom had to sign a suspicious confidentiality agreement
- A jogger who claims that Perry hit on him on the jogging trail
- A New York City policeman who disappears with Perry during a fundraiser

The evidence I've seen and heard convinces me. But of course what I believe matters very little.

For media publication purposes, the standard of proof and the burden of proof are determinative for a story of "this type." That's what has been particularly interesting to me in my convoluted dealings with the journalists who were so interested in publishing the story. What is clear is that ultimately I did not prove the truth of my beliefs to a level that convinced traditional journalistic media (or at least the publisher of one such media outlet) to print the story. At least not yet. As Joey suspected, absent DNA evidence, photos, or tapes, the practical burden of proof remains very high, as does the presumption of untruth. (Ironically, as

Perry's fortunes declined, the burden of proof almost seemed to get higher. Why risk a lawsuit over a has-been candidate?)

And obviously the evidence I found was almost completely hearsay—what someone told me had happened. In matters as private as sex, especially gay sex, that's not surprising. Who collects DNA or takes photos, unless some sort of set-up deal or undercover sting is underway?

But as my lawyer friends have told me, even courts often rely on hearsay evidence. Under Texas law, hearsay that is unobjected to at trial can be adequate to support a jury verdict and a judgment. And the traditional "hearsay rule" is itself subject to several exceptions in a court of law. One exception is a "statement against interest," such as a statement that could subject the speaker to civil or criminal liability. And that presents both a strength and a weakness in any gay hustler's statement.

Sex for money is generally illegal (at least outside of marriage). Why would anyone admit to such conduct unless it was true? But then it's not easy to get someone who engages in such conduct to speak about it on the record.

On the other hand, one point that impressed me about the stories of Joey and James and some of the other sources was that they originally told those stories long before Perry announced for president. Some stories dated back to when Perry was a minor political figure. Those stories had no value at the time, even for bragging or boasting ("Let me tell you about this inconsequential politico I had gay sex with"). Also, they generally told the stories to friends. Do people lie to friends? Sure, sometimes. But generally not.

And for me, some of these stories came from people I've known very well and trusted for many years.

In short, most of these stories I've recounted seem to me to be very believable and to come from very credible people.

Then there's the sheer number of stories, witnesses, and off-hand recollections. As a buddy's Facebook friend said, "I've heard too many stories, first hand kind of stuff, from too many people, some of whom are totally apolitical and have no agenda, not to believe."

Consider that volume of evidence together with the on-the-record sources who spoke to The Journalist.

Has Rick Perry had homosexual relationships? I know what I believe, but you decide for yourself. Perhaps we'll all learn more in the future. For me, searching for the truth has been a very interesting, very frustrating, very illuminating exercise.

About the time I finished writing this book, I went to the store to replace my cell phone. As I chatted with the very handsome twenty-something man who was helping me, I noticed his ring. I asked if it was a college ring. He responded that it was his Army ring, that he had served three tours and then was removed from service.

"I know who you are, and you know why I got kicked out," he said.

He was a victim of Don't Ask Don't Tell, the very policy that Rick Perry has pledged to resurrect if elected President.

At that point the young man was busily moving my phone contacts to the new phone. I mentioned that I had used that phone for lots of text messages with Governor Perry's hustler.

The salesperson nonchalantly said, "My roommate is an older guy just like you. He has a friend who hooked up with Perry."

So it goes.

ABOUT THE AUTHOR

Glen Maxey has worked in Texas politics and with Texas politicians his entire adult life. From 1985, when Rick Perry arrived in Austin, Glen has been an aide to a state senator, the Executive Director and lobbyist for the Lesbian/Gay Rights Lobby of Texas, and served for 12 years as Texas's only openly gay State Representative. He has known Perry as a legislator, Agriculture Commissioner, Lieutenant Governor, and Governor. Glen knows capitol denizens, GLBT folks, lobbyists, politicos, journalists, legislators past and present, and political and gay gossips. That personal history and those personal relationships formed the network of connections that made this book possible.